"JESUS TU...
OF HIS GOO...
THAT, REI...
MANY VAR...
MAN LIFE.'...
—from *WHAT JESUS SAID ABOUT IT*

The teachings of Jesus are as pertinent today as they were almost 2,000 years ago. Now, Henry Koestline has arranged these great words by subjects, for quick reference, in a work as unique as it is useful.

TABLE OF CONTENTS:

Preface ★ *Discipleship* (THE GOOD LIFE) ★ *Eternal Life* ★ *Evangelism* ★ *Faith* ★ *Forgiveness* ★ *God* ★ *Health—Healing* ★ *Himself* ★ *Holy Spirit* ★ *Hypocrites* ★ *Judgment* (HELL, PUNISHMENT) ★ *Kingdom of Heaven* ★ *Love—Brotherhood* (HUMAN RELATIONS) ★ *Marriage—Divorce* ★ *Money* (GIVING, WEALTH) ★ *Passion* (CRUCIFIXION) ★ *Prayer* ★ *Resurrection* ★ *Sin* ★ *Miscellaneous*

WHAT JESUS SAID ABOUT IT

All the words of Jesus in the
New Testament arranged
according to subjects

Henry Koestline

A SIGNET BOOK

NEW AMERICAN LIBRARY

Copyright © 1970 by K. Henry Koestline

All rights reserved

Library of Congress Catalog Card Number: 72-100556

The Bible text in this publication is from the Revised
Standard Version of the Bible, copyrighted 1946 and 1952 by
the Division of Christian Education of the National Council of
the Churches of Christ in the U.S.A. and used by permission.

SIGNET, SIGNET CLASSIC, MENTOR, ONYX, PLUME, MERIDIAN AND NAL
BOOKS are published by NAL Penguin Inc.,
1633 Broadway, New York, New York 10019

First Printing, January, 1970

9   10   11   12   13   14   15   16   17

PRINTED IN CANADA

To
Noel, Allyn, and Kevin

CONTENTS

Preface

The life and teachings of Jesus caused an uproar in the rigid Jewish community of Palestine in the first century. Neither the Roman rulers, eager to keep political peace, nor the Jewish leaders, eager to keep religious peace, were prepared for his coming. No one in authority is prepared for a leader who comes preaching, "Repent, for the kingdom of heaven is at hand."

If, as Bishop Gerald Kennedy suggests, God works in history through a series of explosions, then the coming of Jesus was the greatest explosion of all.

What did Jesus say that stirred the hearts of men and gave them new hope in a time of heavy burdens imposed by religious leaders and the Roman dictatorship?

Jesus referred to his life and teachings as "new wine" which cannot be put into "old wineskins" (Matt. 9:17). When Jesus failed to conform to the popular conception of the Messiah, the crowds crucified him, and his blood flowed like the wine which bursts the old wineskins. The old rigid community could not hold the new life.

What then did he teach that his words are still quoted daily in millions of homes around the world and in hundreds of thousands of pulpits each Sunday?

This little book groups in different subjects all the

words attributed to Jesus in the New Testament. Some scholars deny that Jesus actually said all of these words, and others believe that some of his words have been altered by the writers, translators or editors of the early manuscripts. However, for the purpose of this book, I have included all of the words in the New Testament attributed to him—including those in the Revelation to John.

Jesus undoubtedly spoke many words which were not recorded for us today. As the Gospel of John clearly states (21:25) he did many things in his thirty-three years about which we know nothing. But in the New Testament we have the words considered most important and remembered best by his close followers.

Ellipses (. . .) are frequently used before and after Jesus' words. They indicate that words of another person, or words of the biblical writer have been omitted. In no case have any words of Jesus been omitted.

Preceding the text in each section is a summary of Jesus' teaching on that subject. To understand further the meanings of his words, you should read them in context, in the Bible of your choice. A good Bible commentary will shed additional light on the meaning of these words.

In classifying the sayings of Jesus, I have frequently consulted *The Teachings of Jesus* by Dr. Harvie Branscomb. Of course the final decision on classifying each saying was my own.

Where a particular saying concerns more than one topic, and could not be divided, I have classified the saying in the category which seems to me dominant, while referring to the other subject in boldface. In some cases, the side references are additional topics not included in the subject divisions. For topics not found in the subject headings or margins, the reader is referred to a Bible concordance or Bible dictionary.

The Bible text in this publication is from the Revised Standard Version of the Bible, copyrighted 1946 and

1952 by the Division of Christian Education of the National Council of the Churches of Christ in the U.S.A. and used by permission.

Finally I wish to express appreciation to my teachers of Bible in college and theological seminary who opened many doors for me in the understanding of the Holy Scriptures.

K. Henry Koestline

Miami-Dade Community College
Miami, Florida

WHAT JESUS SAID ABOUT IT

Discipleship

(THE GOOD LIFE)

Four hundred years before Christ, Plato wrote about the good life. Art and beauty, he said, depend on the good. Plato's ideal state included three classes of people, those who were wise, those who were brave, and those who had self-discipline.

Other philosophers, in other times, have described the good life as manmade. Stoics saw the good in devotion to wisdom; hedonists saw it in terms of pleasure.

Jesus' concept of the good life is different. Jesus did not deny pleasure, but he based his description of the good life on something deeper. The good life includes humility, justice, mercy, compassion, and service, all based on love of God and love of fellow man. The happiness of Jesus is actually a paradox; it includes personal freedom and obedience to God.

This chapter includes the many facets of discipleship. Jesus turns the diamond of the good life this way and that, reflecting his light into many, varied corners of human life.

Jesus looked upon the religious life of his beloved people and found it restrictive, superficial, and hypocritical. He proceeded to show them a better way.

Although Jesus was specific in his description of the good life, he was never legalistic. He was not interested in the rules for the sake of keeping rules; he was interested in the good of the individual.

The good life can be summed up by commitment to a Person. "Follow me," he said, "and I will lead you to eternal life." Almost all passages which include the familiar phrase "follow me" are placed in this section.

* * *

Blessed are the poor in spirit, for theirs is the kingdom of heaven.

Blessed are those who mourn, for they shall be comforted.

Blessed are the meek, for they shall inherit the earth.

Blessed are those who hunger and thirst for righteousness, for they shall be satisfied. **happiness**

Blessed are the merciful, for they shall obtain mercy.

Blessed are the pure in heart, for they shall see God.

Blessed are the peacemakers, for they shall be called sons of God.

Blessed are those who are persecuted for righteousness' sake, for theirs is the kingdom of heaven.

Blessed are you when men revile you and persecute you and utter all kinds of evil against you falsely on my account. Rejoice and be glad, for your reward is great in heaven, for so men perse- **reward** cuted the prophets who were before you.

Matt. 5:3-12

Blessed are you poor, for yours is the kingdom of God.

Blessed are you that hunger now, for you shall be satisfied.

Blessed are you that weep now, for you shall laugh.

Blessed are you when men hate you, and when they exclude you and revile you, and cast out your name as evil, on account of the Son of man! Rejoice in that day, and leap for joy, for behold, **reward** your reward is great in heaven; for so their fathers did to the prophets.

But woe to you that are rich, for you have received your consolation.

Woe to you that are full now, for you shall hunger.

Woe to you that laugh now, for you shall mourn and weep.

Woe to you, when all men speak well of you, for so their fathers did to the false prophets.

Luke 6:20-26

You are the salt of the earth; but if salt has lost its taste, how shall its saltness be restored? It is no longer good for anything except to be thrown out and trodden under foot by men.

You are the light of the world. A city set on a hill cannot be hid. Nor do men light a lamp and put it under a bushel, but on a stand, and it gives light to all in the house. Let your light so shine before men, that they may see your good works and give glory to your Father who is in heaven.

Matt. 5:13-16

The eye is the lamp of the body. So, if your eye is sound, your whole body will be full of light; but if your eye is not sound, your whole body will be full of darkness. If then the light in you is darkness, how great is the darkness!

No one can serve two masters; for either he will hate the one and love the other, or he will be devoted to the one and despise the other. You cannot serve God and mammon.

Matt. 6:22-24

Do not give dogs what is holy; and do not throw your pearls before swine, lest they trample them under foot and turn to attack you.

Matt. 7:6

Enter by the narrow gate; for the gate is wide and the way is easy, that leads to destruction, and those who enter by it are many. For the gate is narrow and the way is hard, that leads to life, and those who find it are few.

Matt. 7:13-14

Beware of false prophets, who come to you in sheep's clothing but inwardly are ravenous wolves. You will know them by their fruits. Are grapes gathered from thorns, or figs from thistles? So, every sound tree bears good fruit, but the bad tree bears evil fruit. A sound tree cannot bear evil fruit, nor can **hypocrisy** a bad tree bear good fruit. Every tree that does not bear good fruit is cut down and thrown into the fire. Thus you will know them by their fruits.

Matt. 7:15-20

. . . Follow me, and leave the dead to bury their own dead.

Matt. 8:22

. . . Follow me.

Matt. 9:9

. . . Can the wedding guests mourn as long as the bridegroom is with them? The days will come, when the bridegroom is taken away from them, and then they will fast. And no one puts a piece of unshrunk cloth on an old garment, for the patch tears away from the garment, and a worse tear is made. Neither is new wine put into old wineskins; if it is, the skins burst, and the wine is spilled, and the skins are destroyed; but new wine is put into fresh wineskins, and so both are preserved.

Matt. 9:15-17

. . . Can the wedding guests fast while the bridegroom is with them? As long as they have the bridegroom with them, they cannot fast. The days will come, when the bridegroom is taken away from them, and then they will fast in that day. No one sews a piece of unshrunk cloth on an old garment; if he does, the patch tears away from it, the new from the old, and a worse tear is made. And no one puts new wine into old wineskins; if he does, the wine will burst the skins, and the wine is lost, and so are the skins; but new wine is for fresh skins.

Mark 2:19-22

... Can you make wedding guests fast while the bridegroom is with them? The days will come, when the bridegroom is taken away from them, and then they will fast in those days. ... No one tears a piece from a new garment and puts it upon an old garment; if he does, he will tear the new, and the piece from the new will not match the old. And no one puts new wine into old wineskins; if he does, the new wine will burst the skins and it will be spilled, and the skins will be destroyed. But new wine must be put into fresh wineskins. And no one after drinking old wine desires new; for he says, "The old is good."

Luke 5:34-39

... Come to me, all who labor and are heavy laden, and I will give you rest. Take my yoke upon you, and learn from me; for I am gentle and lowly in heart, and you will find rest for your souls. For my yoke is easy, and my burden is light.

Matt. 11:28-30

... Have you not read what David did, when he was hungry, and those who were with him: how he entered the house of God and ate the bread of the Presence, which it was not lawful for him to eat nor for those who were with him, but only for the priests? Or have you not read in the law how on the sabbath the priests in the temple profane the sabbath, and are guiltless? I tell you, something greater than the temple is here. And if you had known what this means, "I desire mercy, and not sacrifice," you would not have condemned the guiltless. For the Son of man is lord of the sabbath.

Matt. 12:3-8

... Have you never read what David did, when he was in need and was hungry, he and those who were with him: how he entered the house of God, when Abiathar was high priest, and ate the bread of the Presence, which is not lawful for any but the priests to eat, and also gave it to those who were   **sabbath** with him? ... The sabbath was made for man, not man for the sabbath; so the Son of man is lord even of the sabbath.

Mark 2:25-28

... Have you not read what David did when he was hungry, he and those who were with him: how he entered the house of God, and took and ate the bread of the Presence, which it is not   **sabbath** lawful for any but the priests to eat, and also gave it to those with him? ... The Son of man is lord of the sabbath.

Luke 6:3-5

... What man of you, if he has one sheep and it falls into a pit on the sabbath, will not lay hold   **sabbath** of it and lift it out? Of how much more value is a man than a sheep! So it is lawful   **healing** to do good on the sabbath. ... Stretch out your hand.

Matt. 12:11-13

... Come here. ... Is it lawful on the sabbath   **sabbath** to do good or to do harm, to save life or to kill? ... Stretch out your hand.   **healing**

Mark 3:4-5

... Come and stand here. ... I ask you, is it lawful on the sabbath to do good or to do harm,   **sabbath** to save life or to destroy it? ... Stretch out your hand.   **healing**

Luke 6:8-10

. . . Take heed and beware of the leaven of the Pharisees and Sadducees. . . . O men of little faith, why do you discuss among yourselves the fact that you have no bread? Do you not yet perceive? Do you not remember the five loaves of the five thousand, and how many baskets you gathered? Or the seven loaves of the four thousand, and how many baskets you gathered? How is it that you fail to perceive that I did not speak about bread? Beware of the leaven of the Pharisees and Sadducees.

Matt. 16:6-11

. . . If any man would come after me, let him deny himself and take up his cross and follow me. **cross** For whoever would save his life will lose it, and whoever loses his life for my sake will find it. For what will it profit a man, if he gains the whole world and forfeits his life? Or what shall a man give in return for his life? For the Son of man is come with his angels in the glory of his Father, and then he will repay every man for what he has done. Truly, I say to you, there are some standing here who will not taste death before they see the Son of man coming in his kingdom.

Matt. 16:24-28

. . . Rise, and have no fear.

Matt. 17:7

. . . Why do you ask me about what is good? One there is who is good. If you would enter life, keep the commandments. . . . You shall not kill, You shall not commit adultery, You shall not steal, You shall not bear false witness, Honor your father and mother, and, You shall love your neighbor as yourself. . . . If you would be perfect, go, sell what you possess and give to the poor, and you will have treasure in heaven; and come, follow me.

Matt. 19:17-21

. . . Truly, I say to you, in the new world, when the Son of man shall sit on his glorious throne, you who have followed me will also sit on twelve thrones, judging the twelve tribes of Israel. **rewards** And every one who has left houses or brothers or sisters or father or mother or children or lands, for my name's sake, will receive a hundredfold, and inherit eternal life. But many that are first will be last, and the last first.

Matt. 19:28-30

. . . Whoever receives this child in my name receives me, and whoever receives me receives **children** him who sent me; for he who is least among you all is the one who is great.

Luke 9:48

. . . Do not forbid him; for he that is not against you is for you.

Luke 9:50

. . . Foxes have holes, and birds of the air have nests; but the Son of man has nowhere to lay his head. . . . Follow me . . . Leave the dead to bury their own dead; but as for you, go and proclaim **kingdom of God** the kingdom of God. . . . No one who puts his hand to the plow and looks back is fit for the kingdom of God.

Luke 9:58-62

. . . Blessed are the eyes which see what you see! For I tell you that many prophets and kings desired to see what you see, and did not see it, and to hear what you hear, and did not hear it.

Luke 10:23-24

Let your loins be girded and your lamps burning. And be like men who are waiting for their master to come home from the marriage feast, so that they may open to him at once when he comes and knocks. Blessed are those servants whom the master finds awake when he comes; truly, I say to you, he will gird himself and have them sit at table, and he will come and serve them. If he comes in the second watch, or in the third, and finds them so, blessed are those servants! But know this, that if the householder had known at what hour the thief was coming, he would have been awake and would not have left his house to be broken into. You also must be ready; for the Son of man is coming at an hour you do not expect.

Luke 12:35-40

. . . Who then is the faithful and wise steward, whom his master will set over his household, to give them their portion of food at the proper time? Blessed is that servant whom his master when he comes will find so doing. Truly I tell you, he will set him over all his possessions. But if that servant says to himself, "My master is delayed in coming," and begins to beat the menservants and the maidservants, and to eat and drink and get drunk, the master of that servant will come on a day when he does not expect him and at an hour he does not know, and will punish him, and put him with the unfaithful. **punishment** And that servant who knew his master's will, but did not make ready or act according to his will, shall receive a severe beating. But he who did not know, and did what deserved a beating, shall receive a light beating. Every one to whom much is given, of him will much be required; and of him to whom men commit much they will demand the more.

Luke 12:42-48

. . . When you are invited by any one to a marriage feast, do not sit down in a place of honor, lest a more eminent man than you be invited by him; and he who invited you both will come and say to you, "Give place to this man," and then you will begin with shame to take the lowest place. But when you are invited, go and sit in the lowest place, so that when your host comes he may say to you, "Friend, go up higher"; then you will be honored in the presence of all who sit at table with you. For every one who exalts himself will be humbled, and he who humbles himself will be exalted.

Luke 14:8-11

. . . When you give a dinner or a banquet, do not invite your friends or your brothers or your kinsmen or rich neighbors, lest they also invite you in return, and you be repaid. But when you give a feast, invite the poor, the maimed, the lame, the blind, and you will be blessed, because they cannot **reward** repay you. You will be repaid at the resurrection of the just.

Luke 14:12-14

. . . There was a rich man who had a steward, and charges were brought to him that this man was wasting his goods. And he called him and said to him, "What is this that I hear about you? Turn in the account of your stewardship, for you can **stewardship** no longer be steward." And the steward said to himself, "What shall I do, since my master is taking the stewardship away from me? I am not strong enough to dig, and I am ashamed to beg. I have decided what to do, so that people may receive me into their houses when I am put out of the stewardship." So, summoning his master's debtors one by one, he said to the first, "How much do you owe my master?" He said, "A hundred measures of oil." And he said to him, "Take your bill, and sit down quickly and write fifty." Then he said to another, "And how much do you owe?" He said, "A hundred measures of wheat." He said to him, "Take your bill, and write eighty." The master commended the dishonest steward for his prudence; for the sons of this world are wiser in their own generation than the sons of light. And I tell you, make friends for yourselves by means of **stewardship** unrighteous mammon, so that when it fails they may receive you into the eternal habitations.

He who is faithful in a very little is faithful also in much; and he who is dishonest in a very little is dishonest also in much. If then you have not been faithful in the unrighteous mammon, who will entrust to you the true riches? And if you have not been faithful in that which is another's, who will give you that which is your own? No servant can serve two masters; for either he will hate the one and love the other, or he will be devoted to the one and despise the other. You cannot serve God and mammon.

Luke 16:1-13

Will any one of you, who has a servant plowing or keeping sheep, say to him when he has come in from the field, "Come at once and sit down at table"? Will he not rather say to him, "Prepare supper for me, and gird yourself and serve me, till I eat and drink; and afterward you shall eat and drink"? Does he thank the servant because he did what was commanded? So you also, when you have done **humility** all that is commanded you, say, "We are unworthy servants; we have only done what was our duty."

Luke 17:7-10

. . . You know the commandments: "Do not kill, Do not commit adultery, Do not steal, Do not bear false witness, Do not defraud, Honor your father and mother." . . . You lack one thing; go, sell what you have, and give to the poor, and you will have treasure in heaven; and come, follow me.

Mark 10:19-21

. . . You know the commandments: "Do not commit adultery, Do not kill, Do not steal, Do not bear false witness, Honor your father and mother." . . . One thing you still lack. Sell all that you have and distribute to the poor, and you will have trea- **giving** sure in heaven; and come, follow me.

Luke 18:20-22

... A disciple is not above his teacher, but every one when he is fully taught will be like his teacher.

Luke 6:40

... What do you seek? ... Come and see. So you are Simon the son of John? You shall be called Cephas. ... Follow me.

John 1:38-43

... Behold, an Israelite indeed, in whom is no guile! ... Before Philip called you, when you were under the fig tree, I saw you.

John 1:47-48

... Will you also go away? ... Did I not choose you, the twelve, and one of you is a devil?

John 6:67-70

... If you continue in my word, you are truly my disciples, and you will know the truth, and the truth will make you free.

John 8:31-32

Truly, truly, I say to you, he who does not enter the sheepfold by the door but climbs in by another way, that man is a thief and a robber; but he who enters by the door is the shepherd of the sheep. To him the gatekeeper opens; the sheep hear his voice, and he calls his own sheep by name and leads them out. When he has brought out all his own, he goes before them, and the sheep follow him, for they know his voice. A stranger they will not follow, but they will flee from him, for they do not know the voice of strangers.

John 10:1-5

... The hour has come for the Son of man to be glorified. Truly, truly, I say to you, unless a grain of wheat falls into the earth and dies, it remains alone; but if it dies, it bears much fruit. He who loves his life loses it, and he who hates his life in this world will keep it for eternal life. If any one serves me, he must follow me; and where I am, there shall my servant be also; if any one serves me, the Father will honor him.

John 12:23-26

. . . The light is with you for a little longer. Walk while you have the light, lest the darkness overtake you; he who walks in the darkness does not know where he goes. While you have the light, believe in the light, that you may become sons of light.

John 12:35-36

. . . What I am doing you do not know now, but afterward you will understand. . . . If I do not wash you, you have no part in me. . . . He who has bathed does not need to wash, except for his feet, but he is clean all over; and you are clean, but not all of you. . . . You are not all clean.

. . . Do you know what I have done to you? You call me Teacher and Lord; and you are right, for so I am. If I then, your Lord and Teacher, have washed your feet, you also ought to wash one another's feet. For I have given you an example, that you also should do as I have done to you. Truly, truly, I say to you, a servant is not greater than his master; nor is he who is sent greater than he who sent him. If you know these things, blessed are you if you do them.

John 13:7-17

I am the true vine, and my Father is the vine dresser. Every branch of mine that **about himself** bears no fruit, he takes away, and every branch that does bear fruit he prunes, that it may bear more fruit. You are already made clean by the word which I have spoken to you. Abide in me, and I in you. As the branch cannot bear fruit by itself, unless it abides in the vine, neither can you, unless you abide in me. I am the vine, you are the branches. He who abides in me, and I in him, he it is that bears much fruit, for apart from me you can do nothing. If a man does not abide in me, he is cast forth as a branch and withers; and the branches are gathered, thrown into the fire and burned. If you abide in me, and my words abide in you, ask whatever you will, and it shall be done for you. By this my Father is glorified, that you bear much fruit, and so prove to be my disciples.

John 15:1-8

... I am praying for them; I am not praying for the world but for those whom thou hast given **prayer** me, for they are thine; all mine are thine, and thine are mine, and I am glorified in them. And now I am no more in the world, but they are in the world, and I am coming to thee. Holy Father, keep them in thy name, which thou hast given me, that they may be one, even as we are one. While I was with them, I kept them in thy name, which thou hast given me; I have guarded them, and none of them is lost but the son of perdition, that the scripture might be fulfilled. But now I am coming to thee; and these things I speak in the world, that they may have my joy fulfilled in themselves. I have given them thy word; and the world has hated them because they are not of the world, even as I am not of the world. I do not pray that thou shouldst take them out of the world, but that thou shouldst keep them from the evil one. They are not of the world, even as I am not of the world. Sanctify them in the truth; thy word is truth. As thou didst send me into the world, so I have sent them into the world. And for their sake I consecrate myself, that they also may be consecrated in truth.

John 17:9-19

... Peace be with you. ... Peace be with you. As the Father has sent me, even so I send you.   **peace**

John 20:19-21

... Simon, son of John, do you love me more than these? ... Feed my lambs. ... Simon, son of John, do you love me? ... Tend my   **evangelism** sheep. . . . Simon, son of John, do you love me? . . . Feed my sheep. Truly, truly, I say to you, when you were young, you girded yourself and walked where you would; but when you are old, you will stretch out your hands, and another will gird you and carry you where you do not wish to go. . . . Follow me. . . . If it is my will that he remain until I come, what is that to you? Follow me!

John 21:15-22

. . . Do not be afraid, but speak and do not be silent; for I am with you, and no man shall attack you to harm you; for I have many people in this city.

Acts 18:9-10

. . . My grace is sufficient for you, for my power is made perfect in weakness.

II Cor. 12:9

Eternal Life

To Jesus, life here and hereafter was of one cloth. Eternal life begins now, when you commit yourself to him, and continues forever. In the last verse of Matthew's record, Jesus says to his disciples, "I am with you always, even unto the end of the world."

What then? Then, in the minds of early Christians, Christ would remain as friend and Lord after the end of human history. Matthew always looks forward to the great day when Jesus will be visibly present in his heavenly glory to judge the world and say (25:34) "Come, O blessed of my Father, inherit the kingdom prepared for you from the foundation of the world."

Eternal life is not an endless, peaceful existence. It is a quality of life which comes from commitment to the way of Christ. Jesus simply called it "life" as contrasted with the living "death" of those who ignore or refuse his gift of grace. "I am come that they might have life, and that they might have it more abundantly."

When Jesus talked to the loose-living woman of Samaria, he said that the water he gave to mankind shall become "a well of water springing up into eternal life." And he gave her this "living water."

In another passage he uses the symbol of bread instead of water. "I am the living bread . . . if any man eat of this bread, he shall live forever."

The emphasis is on living, now and always. In this perspective, what *we* call death is not an end to life, but a doorway from one room of life to another.

* * *

. . . Truly, I say to you, there is no man who has left house or wife or brothers or parents or children, for the sake of the kingdom of God, who will not receive manifold more in this time, and in **rewards** the age to come eternal life.

Luke 18:29-30

. . . Do not murmur among yourselves. No one can come to me unless the Father who sent me draws him; and I will raise him up at the last day. It is written in the prophets, "And they **resurrection** shall all be taught by God." Every one who has heard and learned from the Father comes to me. Not that any one has seen the Father except him who is from God; he has seen the Father. Truly, truly, I say to you, he who believes has eternal life. I am the bread of life. Your fathers ate the manna in the wilderness, and they died. This is the bread which comes down from heaven, that a man may eat of it and not die. I am the living bread which came down from heaven; if any one eats of this bread, he will live for ever; and the bread which I shall give for the life of the world is my flesh.

John 6:43-51

. . . Truly, truly, I say to you, unless you eat the flesh of the Son of man and drink his blood, you have no life in you; he who eats my flesh and drinks my blood has eternal life, and I will raise him up at the last day. For my flesh is food indeed, and my blood is drink indeed. He who eats my flesh and drinks my blood abides in me, and I in him. As the living Father sent me, and I live because of the Father, so he who eats me will live because of me. This is the bread which came down from heaven, not such as the fathers ate and died; he who eats this bread will live for ever. . . .

. . . Do you take offense at this? Then what if you were to see the Son of man ascending where he was before? It is the spirit that gives life, the flesh is of no avail; the words that I have spoken to you are spirit and life. But there are some of you that do not believe. . . . This is why I told you that no one can come to me unless it is granted him by the Father.

John 6:53-65

. . . My time has not yet come, but your time is always here. The world cannot hate you, but it hates me because I testify of it that its works are evil. Go to the feast yourselves; I am not going up to this feast, for my time has not yet fully come.

John 7:6-8

Evangelism

To carry the gospel to someone else is the compulsion of every Christian in every age. Share the good news! It's too good to keep! Jesus trained his disciples to go and carry the message to others. First, he sent out the twelve, then seventy laymen in pairs into the villages of Palestine. He had given these disciples power to overcome their obstacles and they returned rejoicing. They came back with such enthusiasm that Jesus had to caution them not to rejoice that "the spirits are subject to you, but rather rejoice because your names are written in heaven." That is, your greatest reward is that you are pleasing God.

The same joy comes to the Christian's heart today when he shares his experience of God with others. For his sharing to be neither forced nor contrived, his experience must be genuine.

What instructions did Jesus give his disciples on witnessing to this "pearl of great price"? How did he himself go about talking with those who needed his saving grace? Nicodemus, who was afraid to see Jesus in the daytime and made a night appointment? The Samaritan woman at the well? Or that greedy tax-collector, Zacchaeus?

If we are looking for a formula to use in our own

witnessing, we will not find it, for he talked to each in different ways. The one principle shining through is simply this: He talked to each at his deepest need.

And he did not win them all. As far as we know, the Rich Young Ruler never became a disciple and Jesus was certainly disappointed at this failure. But Jesus was not a salesman going after his annual quota. There is no indication of pressure. He simply helped each one to see himself as he really was, and then offered him eternal life.

* * *

. . . Follow me, and I will make you fishers of men.

Matt. 4:19

. . . Follow me and I will make you become fishers of men.

Mark 1:17

. . . Put out into the deep and let down your nets for a catch. . . . Do not be afraid; henceforth you will be catching men.

Luke 5:4-10

. . . The harvest is plentiful, but the laborers are few; pray therefore the Lord of the harvest to send out laborers into his harvest.

Matt. 9:37-38

. . . Go nowhere among the Gentiles, and enter no town of the Samaritans, but go rather to the lost sheep of the house of Israel. And preach as you go saying, "The kingdom of heaven is at hand." Heal the sick, raise the dead, cleanse lepers, cast **healing** out demons. You received without pay, give without pay. Take no gold, nor silver, nor copper in your belts, no bag for your journey, nor two **money** tunics, nor sandals, nor a staff; for the laborer deserves his food. And whatever town or village you enter, find out who is worthy in it, and stay with him until you depart. As you enter the house, salute it. And if the house is worthy, let your peace come upon it; but if it is not worthy, let your peace return to you. And if any one will not receive you or listen to your words, shake off the dust from your feet as you leave that house or town. Truly, I say to you, it shall be more tolerable on the day of judgment for the land of Sodom and Gomorrah than for that town. **judgment**

Behold, I send you out as sheep in the midst of wolves; so be wise as serpents and innocent as doves. Beware of men; for they will deliver you up to councils, and flog you in their synagogues, and you will be dragged before governors and kings **persecution** for my sake, to bear testimony before them and the Gentiles. When they deliver you up, do not be anxious how you are to speak or what you are to say; for what you are to say will be given to you in that hour; for it is not you who speak, but the Spirit of your Father speaking through you. Brother will deliver up brother to death, and the father his child, and children will rise against parents and have them put to death; and you will be hated by all for my name's sake. But he who endures to the end will be saved. When they persecute you in one town, flee to the next; for truly, I say to you, you will not have gone through all the towns of Israel, before the Son of man comes.

A disciple is not above his teacher, nor a servant above his master; it is enough for the disciple to be like his teacher, and the servant like his master. If they have called the master of **discipleship** the house Be-elzebul, how much more will they malign those of his household.

So have no fear of them; for nothing is covered that will not be revealed, or hidden that will not be known. What I tell you in the dark, utter in the light; and what you hear whispered, proclaim upon the house-tops. And do not fear those who kill the body but cannot kill the soul; rather fear him who can destroy both soul and body in hell. Are not two **hell** sparrows sold for a penny? And not one of them will fall to the ground without your Father's will. But even the hairs of your head are all numbered. Fear not, therefore; you are of more value than many sparrows. So every one who acknowledges me before men, I also will acknowledge before my Father who   **God** is in heaven; but whoever denies me before men, I also will deny before my Father who is in heaven.

Matt. 10:5-33

. . . The harvest is plentiful, but the laborers are few; pray therefore the Lord of the harvest to send out laborers into his harvest. Go your way; behold, I send you out as lambs in the midst of wolves. Carry no purse, no bag, no sandals; and salute no one on the road. Whatever house you enter, first say, "Peace be to this house!" And if a son of peace is there, your peace shall rest upon him; but if not, it shall return to you. And remain in the same house, eating and drinking what they provide, for the laborer deserves his wages; do not go from house to house. Whenever you enter a town and they receive you, eat what is set before you; heal the sick in it and say to them, "The   **healing** kingdom of God has come near to you." But whenever you enter a town and they   **kingdom of** do not receive you, go into its streets and   **God** say,"Even the dust of your town that clings to our feet, we will wipe off against you; nevertheless know this, that the kingdom of God has come near." I tell you, it shall be more tolerable on that day for Sodom than for that town.

Woe to you, Chorazin! woe to you, Beth-saida! for if the mighty works done in you had been done in Tyre and Sidon, they would have repented long ago, sitting in sackcloth and ashes. But it shall be more tolerable in the judgment for Tyre and   **judgment** Sidon than for you. And you, Caperna-um, will you be exalted to heaven? You shall be brought down to Hades.

He who hears you hears me, and he who rejects you rejects me, and he who rejects me rejects him who sent me.

. . . I saw Satan fall like lightning from heaven. Behold, I have given you authority to tread upon serpents and scorpions, and over all the power of the enemy; and nothing shall hurt you. Nevertheless do not rejoice in this, that the spirits **humility** are subject to you; but rejoice that your names are written in heaven.

Luke 10:2-20

. . . He who loves father or mother more than me is not worthy of me; and he who loves son or daughter more than me is not worthy of me; and he who does not take his cross and follow me is **cross** not worthy of me. He who finds his life will lose it, and he who loses his life for my sake will find it.

He who receives you receives me, and he who receives me receives him who sent **brotherhood** me. He who receives a prophet because he is a prophet shall receive a prophet's reward, and he who receives a righteous man because he is a righteous man shall receive a righteous man's reward. And whoever gives to one of these little ones even a **reward** cup of cold water because he is a disciple, truly, I say to you, he shall not lose his reward.

Matt. 10:37-42

. . . Where you enter a house, stay there until you leave the place. And if any place will not receive you and they refuse to hear you, when you leave, shake the dust that is on your feet for a testimony against them.

Mark 6:10-11

. . . Take nothing for your journey, no staff, nor bag, nor bread, nor money; and do not have two tunics. And whatever house you enter, stay there, and from there depart. And wherever they do not receive you, when you leave that town shake off the dust from your feet as a testimony against them.

Luke 9:3-5

A sower went out to sow. And as he sowed, some seeds fell along the path, and the birds came and devoured them. Other seeds fell on rocky ground, where they had not much soil, and immediately they sprang up, since they had no depth of soil, but when the sun rose they were scorched; and since they had no root they withered away. Other seeds fell upon thorns, and the thorns grew up and choked them. Other seeds fell on good soil and brought forth grain, some a hundredfold, some sixty, some thirty. He who has ears, let him hear.

Hear then the parable of the sower. When any one hears the word of the kingdom and does not understand it, the evil one comes and snatches away what is sown in his heart; this is what was sown along the path. As for what was sown on rocky ground, this is he who hears the word and immediately receives it with joy; yet he has no roots in himself, but endures for a while, and when tribulation or persecution arises on account of the word, immediately he falls away. As for what was sown among thorns, this is he who hears the word, but the cares of the world and the delight in riches choke the word, and it proves unfruitful. As for what was sown on good soil, this is he who hears the word and understands it; he indeed bears fruit, and yields, in one case a hundredfold, in another sixty, and in another thirty.

Matt. 13:3-9, 18-23

. . . Listen! A sower went out to sow. And as he sowed, some seed fell along the path, and the birds came and devoured it. Other seed fell on rocky ground, where it had not much soil, and immediately it sprang up, since it had no depth of soil; and when the sun rose it was scorched, and since it had no root it withered away. Other seed fell among thorns and the thorns grew up and choked it, and it yielded no grain. And other seeds fell into good soil and brought forth grain, growing up and increasing and yielding thirtyfold and sixtyfold and a hundredfold. . . . He who has ears to hear, let him hear.

. . . To you has been given the secret of the kingdom of God, but for those outside everything is in parables; so that they may indeed see but not perceive, and may indeed hear but not understand; lest they should turn again, and be forgiven. . . . Do you not understand this parable? How then will you understand all the parables? The sower sows the word. And these are the ones along the path, where the word is sown; when they hear, Satan immediately comes and takes away the word which is sown in them. And these in like manner are the ones sown upon rocky ground, who, when they hear the word, immediately receive it with joy; and they have no root in themselves, but endure for a while; then, when tribulation or persecution arises on account of the word, immediately they fall away. And others are the ones sown among thorns; they are those who hear the word, but the cares of the world, and the delight in riches, and the desire for other things, enter in and choke the word, and it proves unfruitful. But those that were sown upon the good soil are the ones who hear the word and accept it and bear fruit, thirtyfold and sixtyfold and a hundredfold.

Mark 4:3-20

. . . A sower went out to sow his seed; and as he sowed, some fell along the path, and was trodden under foot, and the birds of the air devoured it. And some fell on the rock; and as it grew up, it withered away, because it had no moisture. And some fell among thorns; and the thorns grew with it and choked it. And some fell into good soil and grew, and yielded a hundredfold. . . . He who has ears to hear, let him hear.

. . . To you it has been given to know the secrets of the kingdom of God; but for others they are in parables, so that seeing they may not see, and hearing they may not understand. Now the parable is this: The seed is the word of God. The ones along the path are those who have heard; then the devil comes and takes away the word from their hearts, that they may not believe and be saved. And the ones on the rock are those who, when they hear the word, receive it with joy; but these have no root, they believe for a while and in time of temptation fall away. And as for what fell among the thorns, they are those who hear, but as they go on their way as they are choked by the cares and riches and pleasures of life, and their fruit does not mature. And as for that in the good soil, they are those who, hearing the word, hold it fast in an honest and good heart, and bring forth fruit with patience.

Luke 8:5-15

See that you do not despise one of these little ones; for I tell you that in heaven their angels always behold the face of my Father who is in heaven. What do you think? If a man has a hundred sheep, and one of them has gone astray, does he not leave the ninety-nine on the hills and go in search of the one that went astray? And if he finds it, truly, I say to you, he rejoices over it more than over the ninety-nine that never went astray. So it is not the will of my Father who is in heaven that one of these little ones should perish.

Matt. 18:10-14

And I tell you, every one who acknowledges me before men, the Son of man also will acknowledge before the angels of God; but he who denies me before men will be denied before the angels of God. And every one who speaks a word against **unpardonable sin** the Son of man will be forgiven; but he who blasphemes against the Holy Spirit will not be forgiven. And when they bring you before the synagogues and the rulers and the authorities, do not be anxious how or what you are to answer or what you are to say; for the Holy Spirit will teach **Holy Spirit** you in that very hour what you ought to say.

Luke 12:8-12

. . . What man of you, having a hundred sheep, if he lost one of them, does not leave the ninety-nine in the wilderness, and go after the one which is lost, until he finds it? And when he has found it, he lays it on his shoulders, rejoicing. And when he comes home, he calls together his friends and his neighbors, saying to them, "Rejoice with me, for I have found my sheep which was lost." Just so, I tell you, there will be more joy in heaven over one sinner who repents than over ninety-nine righteous persons who need **joy** no repentance.

Or what woman, having ten silver coins, if she loses one coin, does not light a lamp and sweep the house and seek diligently until she finds it? And when she has found it, she calls together her friends and neighbors, saying, "Rejoice with me, for I have found the coin which I had lost." Just so, I tell you, there is joy before the angels of God over one sinner who repents.

Luke 15:4-10

. . . All authority in heaven and on earth has been given to me. Go therefore and make disciples of all nations, baptizing them in the name of the Father and of the Son and of the Holy Spirit, teaching **teaching** them to observe all that I have commanded you; and lo, I am with you always, to the close of the age.

Matt. 28:18-20

. . . Truly, truly, I say to you, unless one is born anew, he cannot see the kingdom of God . . . Truly, truly, I say to you, unless one is **kingdom of** born of water and the Spirit, he cannot **God** enter the kingdom of God. That which is born of the flesh is flesh, and that which is born of the Spirit is spirit. Do not marvel that I said to you, "You must be born anew." The wind blows where it wills, and you hear the sound of it, but you do not know whence it comes or whither it goes; so it is with every one who is born of the Spirit. . . . Are you a teacher of Israel, and yet you do not understand this? Truly, truly, I say to you, we speak of what we know, and bear witness to what we have seen; but you do not receive our testimony. If I have told you earthly things and you do not believe, how can you believe if I tell you heavenly things? No one has ascended into heaven but he who descended from heaven, the Son of man. And as Moses lifted up the serpent in the wilderness, so must the Son of man be lifted up, that whoever believes in him may have eternal life.

John 3:3, 5-8, 10-15

. . . Give me a drink. . . . If you knew the gift of God, and who it is that is saying to you, "Give me a drink," you would have asked him, and he would have given you living water. . . . Every one who drinks of this water will thirst again, but whoever drinks of the water that I shall give him will never thirst; the water that I shall give him will become in him a spring of water welling up to eternal life. . . .

. . . Go, call your husband, and come here. . . . You are right in saying, "I have no husband," for you have had five husbands, and he **marriage** whom you now have is not your husband; this you said truly. . . . Woman, believe me, the hour is coming when neither on this mountain nor in Jerusalem will you worship the Father. You worship what you do not know; we worship what we know, for salvation is from the Jews. But the hour is coming, and now is, when the true worshipers will worship the Father in spirit and truth, for such the Father seeks to wor-

ship him. God is spirit, and those who worship
him must worship in spirit and truth. . . . I who **God**
speak to you am he.

John 4:7-26

. . . I have food to eat of which you do not know. . . .
My food is to do the will of him who sent me, and to
accomplish his work. Do you not say, "There are yet
four months, then comes the harvest"? I tell you, lift
up your eyes, and see how the fields are already white
for harvest. He who reaps receives wages, and gathers
fruit for eternal life, so that sower and reaper may
rejoice together. For here the saying holds true, "One
sows and another reaps." I sent you to reap that for
which you did not labor; others have labored, and
you have entered into their labor.

John 4:32-38

. . . Truly, truly, I say to you, I am the door of the
sheep. All who came before me are thieves and robbers; but the sheep did not heed them. . . . The thief
comes only to steal and kill and destroy; I came that
they may have life, and have it abundantly. I am the
good shepherd. The good shepherd lays down his life
for the sheep. He who is a hireling and not a shepherd,
whose own the sheep are not, sees the wolf coming
and leaves the sheep and flees; and the wolf snatches
them and scatters them. He flees because he is a hireling and cares nothing for the sheep. I am the good
shepherd; I know my own and my own know me, as
the Father knows me and I know the Father; **himself**
and I lay down my life for the sheep. And I
have other sheep, that are not of this fold; I must bring
them also, and they will heed my voice. So there shall
be one flock, one shepherd. For this reason the Father
loves me, because I lay down my life, that I may take
it again. No one takes it from me, but I lay it down
of my own accord. I have power to lay it down, and

I have power to take it again; this charge I have received from my Father.

John 10:8, 10-18

. . . Saul, Saul, why do you persecute me? . . . I am Jesus, whom you are persecuting; but rise and enter the city, and you will be told what you are to do. . . . . . . Ananias. . . . Rise and go to the street called Straight, and inquire in the house of Judas for a man of Tarsus named Saul; for behold, he is praying, and he has seen a man named Ananias come in and lay his hands on him so that he might regain his sight. . . . Go, for he is a chosen instrument of mine to carry my name before the Gentiles and kings and the sons of Israel; for I will show him how he must suffer for the sake of my name.

Acts 9:4-6, 11-16

. . . Saul, Saul, why do you persecute me? . . . I am Jesus of Nazareth whom you are persecuting. . . . Rise, and go into Damascus, and there you will be told all that is appointed for you to do. . . .
. . . Make haste and get quickly out of Jerusalem, because they will **not** accept your testimony about me. . . .
Depart; for I will send you far away to the Gentiles.

Acts 22:7-10, 18-21

. . . Take courage, for as you have testified about me at Jerusalem, so you must bear witness also at Rome.

Acts 23:11

. . . Saul, Saul, why do you persecute me? It hurts you to kick against the goads. . . . I am Jesus whom you are persecuting. But rise and stand upon your feet; for I have appeared to you for this purpose, to appoint you to serve and bear witness to the things in which you have seen me and to those in which I will appear to you, delivering you from the people and from the

Gentiles—to whom I send you to open their eyes, that they may turn from darkness to light and from the power of Satan to God, that they may receive forgiveness of sins and a place among those who are sanctified by faith in me.

Acts 26:14-18

Faith

Faith is the mainspring of Christian action. The book of Hebrews gives us a classic example: "By faith Abraham . . . went out, not knowing where he was to go." Without faith the Christian is paralyzed. Indeed, without faith can he be a Christian at all?

Jesus had so much faith, such complete faith in the Heavenly Father, that he was constantly amazed at the lack of faith in those around him. His phrase, "O you of little faith," recurs on several occasions. If the people knew the Father as he knew him, they would have faith instead of fear. He commended others for having faith—and usually they were not his disciples.

A reading of the section on healing will reveal the close relationship between faith and healing. Faith is basic not only to healing, but to joy, to prayer, and to power to overcome evil. Faith, Jesus taught, can remove the mountains of despair, of depression, of defeat which so easily beset us, and faith can make us whole, healthy in mind and body.

Jesus manifested his supreme faith when he voluntarily offered himself to the mob in the garden of Gethsemane, knowing that they would crucify him. He trusted that the final victory was in the hands of God. As the book of Hebrews declares: "Now faith is the assurance of things hoped for, the conviction of things not seen."

* * *

Therefore I tell you, do not be anxious about your life, what you shall eat or what you shall drink, nor about your body, what you shall put on. Is not life more than food, and the body more than clothing? Look at the birds of the air: they neither sow nor reap nor gather into barns, and yet your heavenly Father feeds them. Are you not of more value than they? And which of you by being anxious can add one cubit to his span of life? And why are you anxious about cloth- ing? Consider the lilies of the field, how they grow; they neither toil nor spin; yet I tell you, even Solomon in all his glory was not arrayed like one of these. But if God so clothes the grass of the field, which today is alive and tomorrow is thrown into the oven, will he not much more clothe you, O men of little faith? Therefore do not be anxious, saying, "What shall we eat?" or "What shall we drink?" or "What shall we wear?" For the Gentiles seek all these things; and your heavenly Father knows that you need them all. But seek first his kingdom and his righteous- ness, and all these things shall be yours as well.

kingdom of God

Therefore do not be anxious about tomorrow, for tomorrow will be anxious for itself. Let the day's own trouble be sufficient for the day.

Matt. 6:25-34

. . . Why are you afraid, O men of little faith?

Matt. 8:26

. . . Let us go across to the other side. . . . Peace! Be still! . . . Why are you afraid? Have you no faith?

fear

Mark 4:35-40

... Let us go across to the other side of the lake. ...
Where is your faith?

Luke 8:22-25

... Take heart, daughter; your faith has made
you well.

healing

Matt. 9:22

... Who touched my garments? ... Daughter, your
faith has made you well; go in peace, and be healed of
your disease.

Mark 5:30-34

... Who was it that touched me? ... Some one
touched me; for I perceive that power has gone forth
from me. ... Daughter, your faith has made you well;
go in peace.

Luke 8:45-48

... Take heart, it is I; have no fear.
... Come ... O man of little faith, why
did you doubt?

courage

Matt. 14:27-31

... Take heart, it is I; have no fear.

Mark 6:50

... It is I; do not be afraid.

John 6:20

... Because of your little faith. For truly I say to
you, if you have faith as a grain of mustard seed, you
will say to this mountain, "Move hence to yonder
place," and it will move; and nothing will be impossible to you.

Matt. 17:20-21

... What are you discussing with them? ... O faithless generation, how long am I to be with you? How
long am I to bear with you? Bring him to me. ...
How long has he had this? ... If you can! All things

are possible to him who believes. . . . You dumb and deaf spirit, I command you, come out of him, and never enter him again. . . . This kind cannot be driven out by anything but prayer.

Mark 9:16-29

. . . O faithless and perverse generation, how long am I to be with you and bear with you? Bring your son here.

Luke 9:41

. . . If you had faith as a grain of mustard seed, you could say to this sycamine tree, "Be rooted up, and be planted in the sea," and it would obey you.

Luke 17:6

. . . May no fruit ever come from you again! . . . Truly, I say to you, if you have faith and never doubt, you will not only do what has been done to the fig tree, but even if you say to this mountain, "Be taken up and cast into the sea," it will be done. And whatever you ask in prayer, you will receive, if you have faith. **prayer**

Matt. 21:18-22

May no one ever eat fruit from you again. . . .
. . . Have faith in God. Truly, I say to you, whoever says to this mountain, "Be taken up and cast into the sea," and does not doubt in his heart, but believes that what he says will come to pass, **prayer** it will be done for him. Therefore I tell you, whatever you ask in prayer, believe that you receive it, and you will. And whenever you stand praying, **forgiveness** forgive, if you have anything against any one; so that your Father also who is in heaven may forgive you your trespasses.

Mark 11:14, 22-26

. . . Father, into thy hands I commit my spirit! **prayer**

Luke 23:46

. . . It is I; do not be afraid.

John 6:20

. . . If am not doing the works of my Father, then do not believe me; but if I do them, even though you do not believe me, believe the works, that you may know and understand that the Father is in me and I am in the Father.

John 10:37-38

. . . Do you now believe? The hour is coming, indeed it has come, when you will be scattered, every man to his home, and will leave me alone; yet I am not alone, for the Father is with me. I have said this to you, that in me you may have peace. In the peace world you have tribulation; but be of good cheer, I have overcome the world.

John 16:31-33

Forgiveness

Jesus enlarged the concept of forgiveness far beyond that taught by the religion of his time. When Jesus replied to Peter that he was to forgive seventy times seven, he was writing a new chapter in man's understanding of his relationship with his fellow man. Of course, he did not mean for us to keep a record of forgiving until we reach 490, and then reject the person who has injured us. Jesus was dramatically illustrating the unlimited nature of Christian love, rooted in the nature of God. Why forgive? Because God forgives us. It is his nature to forgive and we are to be like him.

All of Christian action is rooted in God, according to Jesus. Thus, he gave no system of philosophy or ethics, but instead kept telling what God is like and asking his disciples to be like him.

Take "forgiveness" for an example. The human reaction to injury is the impulse to retaliate; hurt your enemy who has hurt you. Jesus was convinced, however, that evil can be overcome only with goodness. Man must break the vicious circle of an "eye for an eye" and a "tooth for a tooth." By hurting an enemy, man perpetuates evil; by forgiving him, man ignites goodness.

One of the greatest parables of all, The Prodigal Son,

is in this section. It is the parable of God's forgiving love for sinful man.

* * *

For if you forgive men their trespasses, your heavenly Father also will forgive you; but if you do not forgive men their trespasses, neither will your Father forgive your trespasses.

Matt. 6:14-15

. . . Take heart, my son; your sins are forgiven. . . . Why do you think evil in your hearts? For which is easier, to say, "Your sins are forgiven," or to say, "Rise and walk"? But that you may know that the Son of man has authority on earth to forgive sins. . . . Rise, take up your bed and go home.

Matt. 9:2-6

. . . I do not say to you seven times, but seventy times seven.

Matt. 18:22

. . . Father, forgive them; for they know not what they do.

Luke 23:34

. . . There was a man who had two sons; and the younger of them said to his father, "Father, give me the share of property that falls to me." And he divided his living between them. Not many days later, the younger son gathered all he had and took his journey into a far country, and there he squandered his property in loose living. And when he had spent everything, a great famine arose in that country, and he began to be in want. So he went and joined himself to one of the citizens of that country, who sent him into his fields to feed swine. And he would gladly have fed on the pods that the swine ate; and no one gave him anything. But when he came to himself he said, "How many of my father's hired servants have bread enough and to spare, but I perish here with hunger! I will arise and go to my father, and I will say to him, 'Father, I have sinned against heaven and before you; I am no longer worthy to be called your son; treat me as one of your hired servants.' " And he arose and came to his father. But while he was yet at a distance, his father saw him and had compassion, and ran and embraced him and kissed him. And the son said to him, "Father, I have sinned against heaven and before you; I am no longer worthy to be called your son." But the father said to his servants, "Bring quickly the best robe, and put it on him; and put a ring on his hand, and shoes on his feet; and bring the fatted calf and kill it, and let us eat and make merry; for this my son was dead, and is alive again; he was lost, and is found." And they began to make merry.

Now his elder son was in the field; and as he came and drew near to the house, he heard music and dancing. And he called one of the servants and asked what this meant. And he said to him. "Your brother has come, and your father has killed the fatted calf, because he has received him safe and sound." But he was angry and refused to go in. His father came out and entreated him, but he answered his father, "Lo, these many years I have served you, and I never disobeyed your command; yet you never gave me a kid, that I might make merry with my friends. But when this son of yours came, who has devoured your living with harlots, you killed for him the fatted calf!" And he said to him, "Son, you are always with me, and all that is mine is yours. It was fitting to make merry and be glad, for this your brother was dead, and is alive; he was lost, and is found."

Luke 15:11-32

. . . Take heed to yourselves; if your brother sins, rebuke him, and if he repents, forgive him; and if he sins against you seven times in the day, and turns to you seven times, and says "I repent," you must forgive him.

Luke 17:3-4

God

In a world of visible marvels, faith in the unseen God is difficult for many. Yet everyone lives by faith. We eat in faith that the food set before us is not poisoned. We sleep in faith that the bed will hold us up all night. We love in faith that the one who is the object of our love will respond. We don't *prove* any of these except through experience.

If we could know all about God, he would not be God. That is, no single word, no human understanding, can contain all we mean by the power and majesty of the Supreme Being. Because God is above and beyond our knowing fully, he is sometimes referred to as the "hidden" God.

While God is manifested in nature, and manifested in man, God himself always remains hidden. He is present in the subtleties of life—in relationships of good will, in flashes of creative and constructive insight. But he cannot be seen in the way that a car, a football, or a distant star can be seen.

Thus, we come to understand God—only partially, of course—through symbols. Jesus used the symbol of the father, head of the strongly-knit Jewish family in the Palestinian culture of the first century. The father was a symbol of authority, of love, of discipline. Jesus then used the descriptive noun to mark the distinctive relationship—"Our Father who art in *Heaven*." He is neither male nor female, but encompasses the best characteristics of both genders—not only authority and justice, but compassion and tenderness. Moreover, it is the Christian's faith that God is like Jesus, that Jesus is the best representation of God ever to appear in human form. Thus the Christian doctrine of the incarnation: Jesus is God in the flesh.

In a sense, all of Jesus' teaching is about God. The words of Jesus tell us about the nature of God and how we can follow God's will in our lives. Jesus usually did this in parables. For example, the parable of the Prodigal Son is about the forgiving nature of God. The story is told so that we will know how God loves and forgives us who sin against him. And the implication of the story for our behavior is clear: we are to forgive others in the same way.

Although all of Jesus' words relate in some way to God, the quotations that follow here are those in which Jesus specifically mentions God.

* * *

. . . It is written, "Man shall not live by bread alone, but by every word that proceeds from the mouth of God."
. . . Again it is written, "You shall not tempt the Lord your God." . . . Begone, Satan! for it is written, "You shall worship the Lord your God and him only shall you serve."

Matt. 4:4, 7, 10

. . . It is written, "Man shall not live by bread alone."
. . . It is written, "You shall worship the Lord your God, and him only shall you serve."
. . . It is said, "You shall not tempt the Lord your God."
Luke 4:4, 8, 12

. . . I thank thee, Father, Lord of heaven and earth, that thou hast hidden these things from the wise and understanding and revealed them to babes; yea, Father, for such was thy gracious will. All things have been delivered to me by my Father; and no one knows who the Son is except the Father, or **prayer** who the Father is except the Son and any one to whom the Son chooses to reveal him.

Luke 10:21-22

... I thank thee, Father, Lord of heaven and earth, that thou hast hidden these things from the wise and understanding and revealed them to babes; yea, Father, for such was thy gracious will. **prayer** All things have been delivered to me by my Father; and no one knows the Son except the Father, and no one knows the Father except the Son and any one to whom the Son chooses to reveal him.

Matt. 11:25-27

Therefore the kingdom of heaven may be compared to a king who wished to settle accounts with his servants. When he began the reckoning, one was brought to him who owed him ten **kingdom of** thousand talents; and as he could not **heaven** pay, his lord ordered him to be sold, with his wife and children and all that he had, and payment to be made. So the servant fell on his knees, imploring him, "Lord, have patience with me, and I will pay you everything." And out of pity for him the lord of that servant released him and forgave him the debt. But that same servant, as he went out, came upon one of his fellow servants who owed him a hundred denarii; and seizing him by the throat he said, "Pay what you owe." So his fellow servant fell down and besought him, "Have patience with me, and I will pay you." He refused and went and put him in prison till he should pay the debt. When his fellow servants saw what had taken place, they were greatly distressed, and they went and reported to their lord all that had taken place. Then his lord summoned him and said to him, "You wicked servant!

I forgave you all that debt because you besought me; and should not you have had mercy on your fellow servant, as I had mercy on you?" And in anger his lord delivered him to the jailers, **forgiveness** till he should pay all his debt. So also my heavenly Father will do to every one of you, if you do not forgive your brother from your heart.

Matt. 18:23-35

. . . This is the work of God, that you believe in him whom he has sent.

John 6:29

. . . Even what I have told you from the beginning. I have much to say about you and much to judge; but he who sent me is true, and I declare to the world what I have heard from him. . . . When you have lifted up the Son of man, then you will know that I am he, and that I do nothing on my own authority but speak thus as the Father taught me. And he who sent me is with me; he has not left me alone, for I always do what is pleasing to him.

John 8:25-29

. . . Now is the Son of man glorified, and in him God is glorified; if God is glorified in him, God will also glorify him in himself, and **Himself** glorify him at once.

John 13:31-32

. . . In a certain city there was a judge who neither feared God nor regarded man; and there was a widow in that city who kept coming to him and saying, "Vindicate me against my adversary." For a while he refused; but afterward he said to himself, "Though I neither fear God nor regard man, yet because this widow bothers me, I will vindicate her, or she will wear me out by her continual coming." . . . Hear what the unrighteous judge says. And will not God vindicate his elect, who cry to him day and night? Will he delay long over them? I tell you, he will vindicate them speedily. Nevertheless, when the Son of faith man comes, will he find faith on earth?

Luke 18:2-8

Health—Healing

A study of Jesus' teaching impresses us with his interest in healing the sick. He was not only a teacher and a preacher, he was also a physician.

Because so many persons, ill in body or mind or both, came to him for healing, Jesus had to take care that this aspect of his ministry did not overshadow the others. His primary goal was to reveal the nature and purpose of God to mankind, and to call men to return unto him "that they might have life."

But Jesus was mindful of the fact that God made us to be healthy. A diseased and suffering body works against a healthy spirit; and a sick spirit brings on a sick body. The two cannot be separated. He thus was glad to heal those who came in faith.

Although faith healing has been exploited by the religious charlatans for money and power, this should not blind us to the prominent place of healing in the ministry of Jesus. The church today establishes clinics and hospitals, in the United States and in the mission fields to bring Christ's healing to the sick. Dr. Albert Schweitzer's hospital in Lambarene, Africa, is a classic example of works stemming from Jesus' own concern to heal the sick.

Health, faith, forgiveness of sin, these three are bound together in the teachings of Jesus.

* * *

... I will; be clean. ... See that you say nothing to any one; but go, show yourself to the priest, and offer the gift that Moses commanded, for a proof to the people.

Matt. 8:3-4

... I will; be clean. ... See that you say nothing to any one; but go, show yourself to the priest, and offer for your cleansing what Moses commanded, for a proof to the people.

Mark 1:41-44

... I will; be clean. ... go and show yourself to the priest, and make an offering for your cleansing, as Moses commanded, for a proof to the people.

Luke 5:13-14

... I will come and heal him. ... Truly, I say to you, not even in Israel have I found such faith. I tell you, many will come from east and west and sit at table with Abraham, Isaac, and Jacob in the **faith** kingdom of heaven, while the sons of the kingdom will be thrown into the outer darkness; there men will weep and gnash their teeth. ... Go; be it done for you as you have believed.

Matt. 8:7-13

... I tell you, not even in Israel have I found such faith.

Luke 7:9

... Depart; for the girl is not dead but sleeping.

Matt. 9:24

... Do not fear, only believe. ... Why do you make a tumult and weep? The child is not dead **faith**

but sleeping. . . . Talitha cumi [which means, **death**
Little girl, I say to you, arise].

Mark 5:36-41

. . . Do not fear; only believe, and she shall be well.
. . . Do not weep; for she is not dead but sleeping. . . .
Child, arise.

Luke 8:50-54

. . . Do you believe that I am able to do this? . . .
According to your faith be it done to you. . . . **faith**
See that no one knows it.

Matt. 9:28-30

. . . I was sent only to the lost sheep of the house of
Israel. . . . It is not fair to take the children's bread
and throw it to the dogs. . . . O woman, great is your
faith! Be it done for you as you desire.

Matt. 15:24-28

. . . Let the children first be fed, for it is not right to
take the children's bread and throw it to the dogs. . . .
For this saying you may go your way; the demon has
left your daughter.

Mark 7:27-29

. . . Woman, you are freed from your infirmity.

Luke 13:12

. . . Is it lawful to heal on the sabbath, or not?
. . . Which of you, having an ass or an ox that **sabbath**
has fallen into a well, will not immediately pull him
out on a sabbath day?

Luke 14:3-5

. . . Go and show yourselves to the priests. . . . Were
not ten cleansed? Where are the nine? Was no one
found to return and give praise to God except **faith**
this foreigner? . . . Rise and go your way; your
faith has made you well.

Luke 17:14-19

. . . I have compassion on the crowd, because they have been with me now three days, and have nothing to eat; and I am unwilling to send them away hungry, lest they faint on the way. . . . How many loaves have you?

Matt. 15:32-34

. . . I have compassion on the crowd, because they have been with me now three days, and have nothing to eat; and if I send them away hungry to their homes, they will faint on the way; and some of them have come a long way. . . . How many loaves have you?

Mark 8:2-5

. . . How are we to buy bread, so that these people may eat? . . . Make the people sit down. . . . Gather up the fragments left over, that nothing may be lost.

John 6:5-12

. . . What do you want me to do for you?

Matt. 20:32

. . . What do you want me to do for you? . . . Go your way; your faith has made you well. **faith**

Mark 10:51-52

. . . What do you want me to do for you? . . . Receive your sight; your faith has made you well.

Luke 18:41-42

. . . Unless you see signs and wonders you will not believe. . . . Go; your son will live.

John 4:48-50

. . . Do you want to be healed? . . . Rise, take up your pallet, and walk. . . .
. . . See, you are well! Sin no more, that nothing **sin** worse befall you.

John 5:6-14

. . . This illness is not unto death; it is for the glory of God, so that the Son of God may be glorified by means of it.

... Let us go into Judea again. ... Are there not twelve hours in the day? If any one walks in the day, he does not stumble, because he sees the light of this world. But if any one walks in the night, he stumbles, because the light is not in him. ... Our friend Lazarus has fallen asleep, but I go to awake him out of sleep. ... Lazarus is dead; and for your sake I am glad that I was not there, so that you **resurrection** may believe. But let us go to him. ... Your brother will rise again. ... I am the resurrection and the life; he who believes in me, though he die, yet **life** shall he live, and whoever lives and believes in me shall never die. Do you believe this? ... Where have you laid him? ... **faith** ... Take away the stone. ... Did I not tell you that if you would believe you would see the glory of God? ... Father, I thank thee that thou hast heard me. I knew that thou hearest me always, but I have said this on account of the people standing by, that they may believe that thou didst send me. ... Lazarus, come out. ... Unbind him, and let him go.

John 11:4-44

Himself

Who was this person, healing and teaching throughout Galilee, Samaria, and Judea in the first century? Calling sinners to repentance and preaching the Kingdom of God? "No man spoke like him" testified many who heard him.

Some thought he was Isaiah or Elijah come to life; others conjectured that he was John the Baptist risen from the dead, this man of mighty miracles who spoke with authority.

All the records we have of Jesus' life and teachings were made after his death and resurrection. There was time, then, to get a perspective on his life. Those who followed him closest came to the conclusion that he was the son of God. This was not thin conjecture, but a conclusion based on experience with Jesus as teacher in Palestine and as risen Lord.

This conception of Jesus shows through the gospels and throughout the entire New Testament. This conviction was the motivating force behind the preaching and writing of the letters of Paul which were written even before the gospels were completed. Jesus was Lord, Savior, the long-awaited Christ, the Greek term for the Hebrew, "Messiah."

In his teachings Jesus gave many clues to his own

nature to help his disciples understand who he was. Especially in the gospel of John do we find extensive discourses on his purpose in coming into the world, his relation to the heavenly Father, and his redemptive relationship to man.

There is a mystical quality to these relationships which can best be understood by the use of symbols. Thus Jesus said, "I am the vine, you are the branches." A reading of this section should give us a new appreciation of the place of Jesus in the relationship between God and man.

* * *

Think not that I have come to abolish the law and the prophets; I have come not to abolish them but to fulfil them. For truly, I say to you, till heaven and earth pass away, not an iota, not a dot, will pass from the law until all is accomplished.

Matt. 5:17-18

... Foxes have holes, and birds of the air have nests; but the Son of man has nowhere to lay his head.

Matt. 8:20

... Go and tell John what you hear and see: the blind receive their sight and the lame walk, lepers are cleansed and the deaf hear, and the dead are raised up, and the poor have good news **healing** preached to them. And blessed is he who takes no offense at me.

Matt. 11:4-6

... Go and tell John what you have seen and heard: the blind receive their sight, the lame walk, lepers are cleansed, and the deaf hear, the dead are raised up, the poor have good news preached to them. And blessed is he who takes no offense at me.

Luke 7:22-23

... To you it has been given to know the secrets of the kingdom of heaven, but to them it has not been given. For to him who has will more be given, and he will have abundance; but from him who has giving not, even what he has will be taken away. This is why I speak to them in parables, because seeing they do not see, and hearing they do not hear, nor do they understand. With them indeed is fulfilled the prophecy of Isaiah which says:

> "You shall indeed hear but never understand,
>   and you shall indeed see but never perceive.
> For this people's heart has grown dull,
>   and their ears are heavy of hearing,
>   and their eyes they have closed,
> lest they should perceive with their eyes,
>   and hear with their ears,
> and understand with their heart,
>   and turn for me to heal them."

But blessed are your eyes, for they see, and your ears, for they hear. Truly, I say to you, many prophets and righteous men longed to see what you see, and did not see it, and to hear what you hear, and did not hear it.

Matt. 13:11-17

. . . A prophet is not without honor except in his own country and in his own house.

Matt. 13:57

. . . A prophet is not without honor, except in his own country, and among his own kin, and in his own house.

Mark 6:4

. . . Who do men say that the Son of man is? . . . But who do you say that I am? . . . Blessed are you, Simon Bar-Jona! For flesh and blood has not revealed this to you, but my Father who is in heaven. And I tell you, you are Peter, and on this rock I will build my church, and the powers of death shall not prevail against it. I will give you the keys of the kingdom of heaven, and whatever you bind on earth shall be bound in heaven, and whatever you loose on earth shall be loosed in heaven.

Matt. 16:13-19

. . . Who do men say that I am? . . . But who do you say that I am?

Mark 8:27-29

. . . Who do the people say that I am? . . . But who do you say that I am?

Luke 9:18-20

. . . Elijah does come, and he is to restore all things; but I tell you that Elijah has already come, and they did not know him, but did to him whatever they pleased. So also the Son of man will suffer at their hands.

Matt. 17:11-12

Do not think that I have come to bring peace on earth; I have not come to bring peace, but a sword. For I have come to set a man against his father, and a daughter against her mother, and a daughter-in-law against her mother-in-law; and a man's foes will be those of his own household.

Matt. 10:34-36

I came to cast fire upon the earth; and would that it were already kindled! I have a baptism to be baptized with; and how I am constrained until it is accomplished! Do you think that I have come to give peace on earth? No, I tell you, but rather division; for henceforth in one house there will be five divided, three against two and two against three; they will be divided, father against son and son against father, mother against daughter and daughter against her mother, mother-in-law against her daughter-in-law and daughter-in-law against her mother-in-law.

Luke 12:49-53

. . . Why do you ask me about what is good? One there is who is good. If you would enter life, keep the commandments. **God**

Matt. 19:17

. . . Why do you call me good? No one is good but God alone.

Mark 10:18

. . . Why do you call me good? No one is good but God alone.

Luke 18:19

. . . even as the Son of man came not to be served but to serve, and to give his life as a ransom for many.
Matt. 20:28

. . . For the Son of man also came not to be served but to serve, and to give his life as a ransom for many.
Mark 10:45

. . . I also will ask you a question; and if you tell me the answer, then I also will tell you by what authority I do these things. The baptism of John, whence was it? From heaven or from men? . . . Neither will I tell you by what authority I do these things.

Matt. 21:24-27

. . . I will ask you a question; answer me, and I will tell you by what authority I do these things. Was the baptism of John from heaven or from men? Answer me. . . . Neither will I tell you by what authority I do these things.

Mark 11:29-33

. . . I also will ask you a question; now tell me, Was the baptism of John from heaven or from men? . . . Neither will I tell you by what authority I do these things.

Luke 20:3-8

Hear another parable. There was a householder who planted a vineyard, and set a hedge around it, and dug a wine press in it, and built a tower, and let it out to tenants, and went into another country. When the season of fruit drew near, he sent his servants to the tenants, to get his fruit; and the tenants took his servants and beat one, killed another, and stoned another. Again he sent other servants, more than the first; and they did the same to them. Afterward he sent his son to them, saying, "They will respect my son." But when the tenants saw the son, they said to themselves, "This is the heir; come, let us kill him and have his inheritance." And they took him and cast him out of the vineyard, and killed him. When therefore the owner of the vineyard comes, what will he do to those tenants? . . .

. . . Have you never read in the scriptures: "The very stone which the builders rejected has become the head of the corner; this was the Lord's doing, and it is marvelous in our eyes"? **judgment** Therefore I tell you, the kingdom of God will be taken away from you and given to a nation producing the fruits of it.

Matt. 21:33-44

. . . A man planted a vineyard, and set a hedge around it, and dug a pit for the wine press, and built a tower, and let it out to tenants, and went into another country. When the time came, he sent a servant to the tenants, to get from them some of the fruit of the vineyard. And they took him and beat him, and sent him away empty-handed. Again he sent to them another servant, and they wounded him in the head, and treated him shamefully. And he sent another, and him they killed; and so with many others, some they beat and some they killed. He had still one other, a beloved son; finally he sent him to them, saying, "They will respect my son." But those tenants said to one another, "This is the heir; come, let us **judgment** kill him, and the inheritance will be ours." And they took him and killed him, and cast him out of the vineyard. What will the owner of the vineyard do? He will come and destroy the tenants, and give the vineyard to others. Have you not read this scripture: "The very stone which the builders rejected has become the head of the corner; this was the Lord's doing, and it is marvelous in our eyes"?

Mark 12:1-11

. . . A man planted a vineyard, and let it out to tenants, and went into another country for a long while. When the time came, he sent a servant to the tenants, that they should give him some of the fruit of the vineyard; but the tenants beat him, and sent him away empty-handed. And he sent another servant; him also they beat and treated shamefully, and sent him away empty-handed. And he sent yet a third; this one they wounded and cast out. Then the **judgment** owner of the vineyard said, "What shall I do? I will send my beloved son; it may be they will respect him." But when the tenants saw him, they said to themselves, "This is the heir; let us kill him, that the inheritance may be ours." And they cast him out of the vineyard and killed him. What then will the owner of the vineyard do to them? He will come and destroy those tenants, and give the vineyard to others. . . . What then is this that is written: "The very stone which the builders rejected has become the head of the corner"? Every one who falls on that stone will be broken to pieces; but when it falls on any one it will crush him.

Luke 20:9-18

. . . What do you think of the Christ? Whose son is he? . . . How is it then that David, inspired by the Spirit, calls him Lord, saying, "The Lord said to my Lord, Sit at my right hand, till I put thy enemies under thy feet"? If David thus calls him Lord, how is he his son?

Matt. 22:42-45

. . . How can the scribes say that the Christ is the son of David? David himself, inspired by the Holy Spirit, declared, "The Lord said to my Lord, Sit at my right hand, till I put thy enemies under thy feet." David himself calls him Lord; so how is he his son?

Mark 12:35-37

. . . How can they say that the Christ is David's son? For David himself says in the Book of Psalms, "The Lord said to my Lord, Sit at my right hand, till I make thy enemies a stool for thy feet." David thus calls him Lord; so how is he his son?

Luke 20:41-44

. . . Because I said to you, I saw you under the fig tree, do you believe? You shall see greater things than these. . . . Truly, truly, I say to you, you will see heaven opened, and the angels of God ascending and descending upon the Son of man.

John 1:50:51

. . . My Father is working still, and I am working. . . . . . . Truly, truly, I say to you, the Son can do nothing of his own accord, but only what he sees the Father doing; for whatever he does, that the Son does likewise. For the Father loves the Son, and shows him all that he himself is doing; and greater works **God** than those will he show him, that you may marvel. For as the Father raises the dead and gives them life, so also the Son gives life to whom he will. The Father judges no one, but has given all judgment to the Son, that all may honor the Son, even as they honor the Father. He who does not honor the Son does not honor the Father who sent him. Truly, truly, I say to you, he who hears my word and believes him who sent me, has eternal life; he does not come into judgment, but has passed from death to life.

Truly, truly, I say to you, the hour is coming, and now is, when the dead will hear the voice of the Son of God, and those who hear will live. For as the Father has life in himself, so he has granted the Son also to have life in himself, and has given him au- **life** thority to execute judgment, because he is the Son of man. Do not marvel at this; for the hour is coming when all who are in the tombs will hear his voice and come forth, those who have done good, to the resurrection of life, and those who have done evil, to the resurrection of judgment.

I can do nothing on my own authority; as I hear, I judge; and my judgment is just, because I seek not my own will but the will of him who sent **God** me. If I bear witness to myself my testimony is not true; there is another who bears witness to me and I know that the testimony which he bears to me is true. You sent to John, and he has borne witness to the truth. Not that the testimony which I receive is from man; but I say this that you may be saved. He was a burning and shining lamp, and you were willing to rejoice for a while in his light. But the testimony which I have is greater than that of John; for the works which the Father has granted me to accomplish, these very works which I am doing, **salvation** bear me witness that the Father has sent me. And the Father who sent me has himself borne witness to me. His voice you have never heard, his form you have never seen; and you do not have his word abiding in you, for you do not believe him whom he has sent. You search the scriptures, because you think that in them you have eternal life; and it is they that bear witness to me; yet you refuse to come to me **life** that you may have life. I do not receive glory from men. But I know that you have not the love of God within you. I have come in my Father's name, and you do not receive me; if another comes in his own name, him you will receive. How can you believe, who receive glory from one another and do not seek the glory that comes from the only God? Do not think that I shall accuse you to the Father; it is **God** Moses who accuses you, on whom you set your hope. If you believed Moses, you would believe me, for he wrote of me. But if you do not believe his writings, how will you believe my words?

John 5:17-47

... Truly, truly, I say to you, it was not Moses who gave you the bread from heaven; my Father gives you the true bread from heaven. For the bread of God is that which comes down from heaven, and gives life to the world. ...

... I am the bread of life; he who comes to me shall not hunger, and he who believes in me shall never thirst. But I said to you that you have seen me and yet do not believe. All that the Father gives me will come to me; and him who **salvation** comes to me I will not cast out. For I have come down from heaven, not to do my own will, but the will of him who sent me; and this is the will of him **life** who sent me, that I should lose nothing of all that he has given me, but raise it up at the last day. For this is the will of my Father, that every one who sees the Son and believes **resurrection** in him should have eternal life; and I will raise him up at the last day.

John 6:32-40

... My time has not yet come, but your time is always here. The world cannot hate you, **passion** but it hates me because I testify of it that its works are evil. Go to the feast yourselves; I am not going up to this feast, for my time has not yet fully come.

John 7:6-8

... My teaching is not mine, but his who sent me; if any man's will is to do his will, he shall know **God** whether the teaching is from God or whether I am speaking on my own authority. He who speaks on his own authority seeks his own glory; but he who seeks the glory of him who sent him is true, and in him there is no falsehood. Did not Moses give you the law? Yet none of you keeps the law. Why do you seek to kill me? . . . I did one deed, and you all marvel at it. Moses gave you circumcision (not that it is from Moses, but from the fathers), and you circumcise a man upon the sabbath. If on **hypocrisy** the sabbath a man receives circumcision, so that the law of Moses may not be broken, are you angry with me because on the sabbath I made a man's whole body well? Do not judge by appear- **judgment** ances, but judge with right judgment.

John 7:16-24

. . . You know me, and you know where I come from? But I have not come of my own accord; he who sent me is true, and him you do not know. I know him, for I come from him, and he sent me. . . .
. . . I shall be with you a little longer, and then I go to him who sent me; you will seek me and you will not find me; where I am you cannot come. . . .
. . . If any one thirst, let him come to me and drink. He who believes in me, as the scripture has said, "Out of his heart shall flow rivers of living water."

John 7:28-38

. . . I am the light of the world; he who follows me will not walk in darkness, but will have the light of life. . . . Even if I do bear witness to myself, my testimony is true, for I know whence I have come and whither I am going, but you do not know whence I come or whither I am going. You judge according to the flesh, I judge no one. Yet even if I do judge, my judgment is true, for it is not I alone that judge, but I and he who sent me. In your **judgment** law it is written that the testimony of two men is true; I bear witness to myself, and the Father who sent me bears witness to me. . . . You know neither me nor my Father; if you knew me, you would know **God** my Father also. . . .

John 8:12-19

. . . If I glorify myself, my glory is nothing; it is my Father who glorifies me, of whom you say that he is your God. But you have not known him; I know him. If I said, I do not know him, I should be a liar like you; but I do know him and I keep his word. Your father Abraham rejoiced that he was to see my day; he saw it and was glad. . . . Truly, truly, I say to you, before Abraham was, I am.

John 8:54-58

. . . Do you believe in the Son of man? . . . You have seen him, and it is he who speaks to you. . . .

John 9:35-37

. . . Truly, truly, I say to you, I am the door of the sheep. . . . I am the door; if any one enters by me, he will be saved, and will go in and out and find pasture.

John 10:7-9

. . . I told you, and you do not believe. The works that I do in my Father's name, they bear witness to me; but you do not believe, because you do not belong to my sheep. My sheep hear my voice, and I know them, and they follow me; and I give them eternal life, and they shall never perish, and no one shall snatch them out of my hand. My Father, who has given them to me, is greater than all, and no one is able to snatch them out of the Father's hand. I and the Father are one.

. . . I have shown you many good works from the Father; for which of these do you stone me? . . . Is it not written in your law, "I said, you are gods"? If he called them gods to whom the word of God came (and scripture cannot be broken), do you say of him whom the Father consecrated and sent into the world, "You are blaspheming," because I said, "I am the Son of God"?

John 10:25-36

. . . This voice has come for your sake, not for mine. Now is the judgment of this world, now shall the ruler of this world be cast out; **judgment** and I, when I am lifted up from the earth, will draw all men to myself.

John 12:30-32

. . . I am the way, and the truth, and the life; **life** no one comes to the Father, but by me. If you had known me, you would have known my Father also; henceforth you know him and have seen him. . . . Have I been with you so long, and yet you do not know me, Philip? He who has seen me has seen the Father; how can you say, "Show us the Father"? Do you not believe that I am in the Father and the Father in me? The words that I say to you I do not speak on my own authority; but the Father who dwells in me does his works. Believe me that I am in the Father and the Father in me; or else believe me for the sake of the works themselves.

Truly, truly, I say to you, he who believes in me will also do the works that I do; and greater works than these will he do, because I go to the Father. . . .

John 14:6-12

A little while, and you will see me no more; again a little while, and you will see me. . . . Is this what you are asking yourselves, what I meant by saying, "A little while, and you will not see me, and again a little while, and you will see me"? Truly, truly, I say to you, you will weep and lament, but the world will rejoice; you will be sorrowful, but your sorrow **joy** will turn into joy. When a woman is in travail she has sorrow, because her hour has come; but when she is delivered of the child, she no longer remembers the anguish, for joy that a child is born into the world. So you have sorrow now, but I will see you again and your hearts will rejoice, and no one will take your joy from you. In that day you will ask nothing of me.

Truly, truly, I say to you, if you ask anything of the Father, he will give it to you in my name. Hitherto you have asked nothing in my name; **prayer** ask, and you will receive, that your joy may be full.

I have said this to you in figures; the hour is coming when I shall no longer speak to you in figures but tell you plainly of the Father. In that day you will ask in my name; and I do not say to you that I shall pray the Father for you; for the Father himself **love** loves you, because you have loved me and have believed that I came from the Father. I came from the Father and have come into the world; again, **God** I am leaving the world and going to the Father.

John 16:16-28

. . . Father, the hour has come; glorify thy Son that the Son may glorify thee, since thou hast given him power over all flesh, to give eternal life to all whom thou hast given him. And this is eternal life, that they know thee the only **eternal life** true God, and Jesus Christ whom thou hast sent. I glorified thee on earth, having accomplished the work which thou gavest me to do; and now, Father, glorify thou me in thy own presence with the glory which I had with thee before the world was made.

I have manifested thy name to the men whom thou gavest me out of the world; thine they were, and thou gavest them to me, and they have kept thy word. Now they know that everything that thou hast given me is from thee; for I have given them the words which thou gavest me, and they have received them and know in truth that I came from thee; and they have believed that thou didst send me.

John 17:1-8

Holy Spirit

Almost all of Jesus' teaching about the Holy Spirit is found in the gospel of John. According to Jesus the Holy Spirit is the Comforter, the Spirit of Truth. The Holy Spirit comes after Jesus goes away, and remains with us and guides us "into all truth."

Jesus gives no theological definition of the Holy Spirit, as some of the early church creeds try to do. He says "The Holy Spirit, whom the Father will send in my name." The earlier form in English, Holy Ghost, is often replaced today by Holy Spirit because of the misleading, spectral connotations of "ghost." The *original* Greek word means "wind" or "spirit."

In the Apostle's Creed, which millions of Christians recite every Sunday, the words appear, "I believe in the Holy Spirit (Ghost)." Perhaps the Holy Spirit, like so much of Christianity, cannot be understood until he is experienced. Certainly the early Christians, including the writers of the New Testament, experienced him first; then they set about trying to write down who he is and what his part is in the great drama of the Christian faith.

We look upon the Holy Spirit as God's Spirit in everyday action.

* * *

If you love me, you will keep my commandments. And I will pray the Father, and he will give you another Counselor, to be with you for ever, even **love** the Spirit of truth, whom the world cannot receive, because it neither sees him nor knows him; you know him, for he dwells with you, and will be in you.

I will not leave you desolate; I will come to you. Yet a little while, and the world will see me no more, but you will see me; because I live, you will live also. In that day you will know **eternal life** that I am in my Father, and you in me, and I in you. He who has my commandments and keeps them, he it is who loves me; and he who loves me will be loved by my Father, and I will love him and manifest myself to him. . . . If a man loves me, he will keep my word, and my Father will love him, and we will **love** come to him and make our home with him. He who does not love me does not keep my words; and the word which you hear is not mine but the Father's who sent me.

These things I have spoken to you, while I am still with you. But the Counselor, the Holy Spirit, whom the Father will send in my name, he will teach you all things, and bring to your remembrance all that I have said to you.

John 14:15-26

. . . But when the Counselor comes, whom I shall send to you from the Father, even the Spirit of truth, who proceeds from the Father, he will bear witness to me; and you also are witnesses, because you have been with me from the beginning.

I have said all this to you to keep you from falling away. They will put you out of the synagogues; indeed, the hour is coming when whoever kills you will think he is offering service to **persecution** God. And they will do this because they have not known the Father, nor me. But I have said these things to you, that when their hour comes you may remember that I told you of them.

I did not say these things to you from the beginning, because I was with you. But now I am going to him who sent me; yet none of you asks me, "Where are you going?" But because I have said these things to you, sorrow has filled your hearts. Nevertheless, I tell you the truth: it is to your advantage that I go away, for if I do not go away, the Counselor will not come to you; but if I go, I will send him to you. And when he comes, he will convince the world of sin and of righteousness and of judgment: of sin, because they do not believe in me; of righteousness, because I go to the Father, and you will see me no more; of judgment, because the ruler of this world is judged.

I have yet many things to say to you, but you cannot bear them now. When the Spirit of truth comes, he will guide you into all the truth; for he will not speak on his own authority, but whatever he hears he will speak, and he will declare to you the things that are to come. He will glorify me, for he will take what is mine and declare it to you. All that the Father has is mine; therefore I said that he will take what is mine and declare it to you.

John 15:26-27, 16:1-15

. . . Receive the Holy Spirit. If you forgive the sins of any, they are forgiven; if you retain the sins of any, they are retained.

John 20:22-23

. . . you heard from me, for John baptized with water, but before many days you shall be baptized with the Holy Spirit.
. . . It is not for you to know times or seasons which the Father has fixed by his own authority. But you shall receive power when the Holy Spirit has come upon you; and you shall be my witnesses in Jerusalem and in all Judea and Samaria and to the end of the earth.

Acts 1:4-8

. . . John baptized with water, but you shall be baptized with the Holy Spirit.

Acts 11:16

Hypocrites

Jesus reserved his strongest words of condemnation for the hypocrites, those who were proud of their righteousness, those who paraded their goodness so all could see, those who kept the letter of the law and ignored the spirit.

Jesus prized humility. Those hypocrites who lacked it lacked his spirit, and Jesus condemned them far more severely than he condemned the tax-collectors, the prostitutes, the violent.

Hypocrisy is a more subtle sin than most. The fruit of pride, which some theologians say is the root of all sin, hypocrisy is especially dangerous, for it undermines the good which Jesus and his church stand for today.

* * *

And when you fast, do not look dismal, like the hypocrites, for they disfigure their faces that their fasting may be seen by men. Truly, I say to you, they have their reward. But when you fast, anoint your head and wash your face, that your fasting may not be seen by men but by your Father who is in secret; and your Father who sees in secret will reward you.

Matt. 6:16-18

. . . Why do you see the speck that is in your brother's eye, but do not notice the log that is in your own eye? Or how can you say to your brother, "Let me take the speck out of your eye," when there is the log in your own eye? You hypocrite, first take the log out of your own eye, and then you will see clearly to take the speck out of your brother's eye.

Matt. 7:3-5

What do you think? A man had two sons; and he went to the first and said, "Son, go and work in the vineyard today." And he answered, "I will not"; but afterward he repented and went. And he went to the second and said the same; and he answered, "I go, sir," but did not go. Which of the two did the will of his father? . . . Truly, I say to you, the tax collectors and the harlots go into the kingdom of God before you. For John came to you in the way of righteousness, and you did not believe him, but the tax collectors and the harlots believed him; and even when you saw it, you did not afterward repent and believe him.

Matt. 21:28-32

. . . The scribes and the Pharisees sit on Moses' seat; so practice and observe whatever they tell you, but not what they do; for they preach, but do not practice. They bind heavy burdens, hard to bear, and lay them on men's shoulders; but they themselves will not move them with their finger. They do all their deeds to be seen by men; for they make their phylacteries broad and their fringes long, and they love the place of honor at feasts and the best seats in the synagogues, and salutations in the market places, and being called rabbi by men. But you are not to be called rabbi, for you have one teacher, and you are all brethren. And call no man your father on earth, for you have one Father, who is in heaven. Neither be called masters, for you have one master, the Christ. He who is greatest among you shall be your servant; whoever exalts himself will be humbled, and whoever humbles himself will be exalted.

But woe to you, scribes and Pharisees, hypocrites! because you shut the kingdom of heaven against men; for you neither enter yourselves, nor allow those who would enter to go in. Woe to you, scribes and Pharisees, hypocrites! for you traverse sea and land to make a single proselyte, and when he becomes a proselyte, you make him twice as much a child of hell as yourselves.

Woe to you, blind guides, who say, "If any one swears by the temple, it is nothing; but if any one swears by the gold of the temple, he is bound by his oath." You blind fools! For which is greater, the gold or the temple that has made the gold sacred? And you say, "If any one swears by the altar, it is nothing; but if any one swears by the gift that is on the altar, he is bound by his oath." You blind men! For which is greater, the gift or the altar that makes the gift sacred? So he who swears by the altar, swears by it and by everything on it; and he who swears by the temple, swears by it and by him who dwells in it; and he who swears by heaven, swears by the throne of God and by him who sits upon it.

Woe to you, scribes and Pharisees, hypocrites! for you tithe mint and dill and cummin, and have neglected the weightier matters of the law, justice and mercy and faith; these you ought to have done, without neglecting the others. You blind guides, straining out a gnat and swallowing a camel!

Woe to you, scribes and Pharisees, hypocrites! for you cleanse the outside of the cup and of the plate, but inside they are full of extortion and rapacity. You blind Pharisees! first cleanse the inside of the cup and of the plate, that the outside also may be clean.

Woe to you, scribes and Pharisees, hypocrites! for you are like whitewashed tombs, which outwardly appear righteous to men, but within you are full of hy-bones and all uncleanness. So you also outwardly appear righteous to men, but within you are full of hypocrisy and iniquity.

Woe to you, scribes and Pharisees, hypocrites! for you build the tombs of the prophets and adorn the monuments of the righteous, saying, "If we had lived in the days of our fathers, we would not have taken part with them in shedding the blood of the prophets." Thus you witness against yourselves, that you are sons of those who murdered the prophets. Fill up, then, the measure of your fathers. You serpents, you brood of vipers, how are you to escape being sentenced to hell? Therefore I send you prophets and wise men and scribes, some of whom you will kill and crucify, **hell** and some you will scourge in your synagogues and persecute from town to town, that upon you may come all the righteous blood shed on earth, from the blood of innocent Abel to the blood of Zechariah the son of Barachiah, whom you murdered **judgment** between the sanctuary and the altar. Truly, I say to you, all this will come upon this generation.

Matt. 23:2-36

. . . Beware of the scribes, who like to go about in long robes, and to have salutations in the market places and the best seats in the synagogues and the places of honor at feasts, who devour widows' houses and for a pretense make long prayers. They will receive the greater condemnation.

Mark 12:38-40

. . . Now you Pharisees cleanse the outside of the cup and of the dish, but inside you are full of extortion and wickedness. You fools! Did not he who made the outside make the inside also? But give for alms those things which are within; and behold, everything is clean for you.

But woe to you Pharisees! for you tithe mint and rue and every herb, and neglect justice and the love of God; these you ought to have done, without neglecting the others. Woe to you Pharisees! for you love the best seat in the synagogues and salutations in the market places. Woe to you! for you are like graves which are not seen, and men walk over them without knowing it.

Luke 11:39-44

. . . Beware of the leaven of the Pharisees, which is hypocrisy. Nothing is covered up that will not be revealed, or hidden that will not be known. Whatever you have said in the dark shall be heard in the light, and what you have whispered in private rooms shall be proclaimed upon the housetops.

I tell you, my friends, do not fear those who kill the body, and after that have no more that they can do. But I will warn you whom to fear: fear **death** him who, after he has killed, has power to cast into hell; yes, I tell you, fear him! Are not five sparrows sold for two pennies? And not one of them **hell** is forgotten before God. Why, even the hairs of your head are all numbered. Fear not; you are **God** of more value than many sparrows. **fear**

Luke 12:1-7

. . . When you see a cloud rising in the west, you say at once, "A shower is coming"; and so it happens. And when you see the south wind blowing, you say, "There will be scorching heat"; and it happens. You hypocrites! You know how to interpret the appearance of earth and sky; but why do you not know how to interpret the present time?

And why do you not judge for yourselves what is right?

Luke 12:54-57

. . . You hypocrites! Does not each of you on the sabbath untie his ox or his ass from the manger, and lead it away to water it? And ought not this woman, a daughter of Abraham whom Satan bound for eighteen years, be loosed from this bond on the sabbath day?

Luke 13:15-16

. . . Beware of the scribes, who like to go about in long robes, and love salutations in the market places and the best seats in the synagogues and the places of honor at feasts, who devour widows' houses and for a pretense make long prayers. They will receive the greater condemnation.

Luke 20:46-47

Judgment

(HELL, PUNISHMENT)

Jesus made this clear in his teaching: judgment is real. There is a time of accounting for everyone. We reap what we sow. "You can't plant thistles and reap strawberries," Henry Hitt Crane said in regard to making peace instead of war, but the principle applies to every area of life.

We live in an orderly universe of cause and effect. Sooner or later our sins will find us out and destroy us. There is judgment in the universe. God does not want us to be destroyed by sin, and he has worked through prophets—of old and modern times—to warn us we must love or perish. Finally, he sent Jesus.

In the gospel of John, Jesus made it clear that he is not the one who judges—he came to save the world, not judge it; but there is one who does judge, "the Father who sent me."

The purpose of judgment is not to destroy, but to save. Judgment is necessary to teach us the better way, the way to God, but Jesus comes that we may receive rewards and not punishment.

* * *

Not every one who says to me, "Lord, Lord," shall enter the kingdom of heaven, but he who does the will of my Father who is in heaven. On that day many will say to me, "Lord, Lord, did we not prophesy in your name, and cast out demons in your name, and do many mighty works in your name? And then I will declare to them, 'I never knew you; depart from me, you evildoers.' "

Every one then who hears these words of mine and does them will be like a wise man who built his house upon the rock; and the rain fell, and the floods came, and the winds blew and beat upon that house, but it did not fall, because it had been founded on the rock. And every one who hears these words of mine and does not do them will be like a foolish man who built his house upon the sand; and the rain fell, and the floods came, and the winds blew and beat against that house, and it fell; and great was the fall of it.

Matt. 7:21-27

Why do you call me "Lord, Lord," and not do what I tell you? Every one who comes to me and hears my words and does them, I will show you what he is like: he is like a man building a house, who dug deep, and laid the foundation upon rock; and when a flood arose, the stream broke against that house, and could not shake it, because it had been well built. But he who hears and does not do them is like a man who built a house on the ground without a foundation; against which the stream broke, and immediately it fell, and the ruin of that house was great.

Luke 6:46-49

. . . Woe to you lawyers also! for you load men with burdens hard to bear, and you yourselves do not touch the burdens with one of your fingers. Woe **hypocrisy** to you! for you build the tombs of the prophets whom your fathers killed. So you are witnesses and consent to the deeds of your fathers; for they killed them, and you build their tombs. Therefore also the Wisdom of God said, "I will send them prophets and apostles, some of whom they will kill and persecute," that the blood of all the prophets, shed from the foundation of the world, may be required of this generation, from the blood of Abel to the blood of Zechariah, who perished between the altar and the sanctuary. Yes, I tell you, it shall be required of this generation. Woe to you lawyers! for you have taken away the key of knowledge; and did not enter yourselves, and you hindered those who were entering.

Luke 11:46-52

. . . A man had a fig tree planted in his vineyard; and he came seeking fruit on it and found none. And he said to the vinedresser, "Lo, these three years I have come seeking fruit on this fig tree, and I find none. Cut it down; why should it use up the ground?" And he answered him, "Let it alone, sir, this year also, till I dig about it and put on manure. And if it bears fruit next year, well and good; but if not, you can cut it down."

Luke 13:6-9

. . . Strive to enter by the narrow door; for many, I tell you, will seek to enter and will not be able. When once the householder has risen up and shut the door, you will begin to stand outside and to knock at the door, saying, "Lord, open to us." He will answer you, "I do not know where you come from." Then you will begin to say, "We ate and drank in your presence, and you taught in our streets." But he will say, "I tell you, I do not know where you come from; depart from me, all you workers of iniquity!" There you will weep and gnash your teeth, when you see Abraham and Isaac and Jacob and all the prophets in the kingdom of God and you yourselves thrust out. And men will come from east and west, and from north and south, and sit at table in the kingdom of God. And behold, some are last who will be first, and some are first who will be last.

Luke 13:24-30

. . . The days are coming when you will desire to see one of the days of the Son of man, and you will not see it. And they will say to you, "Lo, there!" or "Lo, here!" Do not go, do not follow them. For as the lightning flashes and lights up the sky from one side to the other, so will the Son of man be in his day. But first he must suffer many things and be rejected by this generation. As it was in the days of Noah, so will it be in the days of the Son of man. They ate, they drank, they married, they were given in marriage, until the day when Noah entered the ark, and the flood came and destroyed them all. Likewise as it was in the days of Lot—they ate, they drank, they bought, they sold, they planted, they built, but on the day when Lot went out from Sodom fire and brimstone rained from heaven and destroyed them all—so will it be on the day when the Son of man is revealed. On that day, let him who is on the housetop, with his goods in the house, not come down to take them away; and likewise let him who is in the field not turn back. Remember Lot's wife. Whoever seeks to gain his life will lose it, but whoever loses his life will preserve it. I tell you, in that night there will be two men in one bed; one will be taken and the other left. There will be two women grinding together; one will be taken and the other left. . . . Where the body is, there the eagles will be gathered together.

Luke 17:22-37

. . . Take heed that no one leads you astray. For many will come in my name, saying, "I am the Christ," and they will lead many astray. And you will hear of wars and rumors of wars; see that you are not alarmed; for this must take place, but the end is not yet. For nation will rise against nation, and kingdom against kingdom, and there will be famines and earthquakes in various places: all this is but the beginning of the sufferings.

Then they will deliver you up to tribulation, and put you to death; and you will be hated by all nations for my name's sake. And then many will fall away, and betray one another, and hate one another. And many false prophets will arise and lead many astray. And because wickedness is multiplied, most men's love will grow cold. But he who endures to the end will be saved. And this gospel of the kingdom will be preached throughout the whole world, as a testimony to all nations; and then the end will come.

So when you see the desolating sacrilege spoken of by the prophet Daniel, standing in the holy place (let the reader understand), then let those who are in Judea flee to the mountains; let him who is on the housetop not go down to take what is in his house; and let him who is in the field not turn back to take his mantle. And alas for those who are with child and for those who give suck in those days! Pray that your flight may not be in winter or on a sabbath. For then there will be great tribulation, such as has not been from the beginning of the world until now, no and never will be. And if those days had not been shortened, no human being would be saved; but for the sake of the elect those days will be shortened. Then if any one says to you, "Lo, here is the Christ!" or "There he is!" do not believe it. For false Christs and false prophets will arise and show great signs and wonders, so as to lead astray, if possible, even the elect. Lo, I have told you beforehand. So, if they say to you, "Lo, he is in the wilderness," do not go out; if they say, "Lo, he is in the inner rooms," do not believe it. For as the lightning comes from the east and shines as far as the west, so will be the coming of the Son of man. Wherever the body is, there the eagles will be gathered together.

Immediately after the tribulation of those days the sun will be darkened, and the moon will not give its light, and the stars will fall from heaven, and the powers of the heavens will be shaken; then will appear the sign of the Son of man in heaven, and then all the tribes of the earth will mourn, and they will see the Son of man coming on the clouds of heaven with power and great glory; and he will send out his angels with a loud trumpet call, and they will gather his elect from the four winds, from one end of heaven to the other.

From the fig tree learn its lesson: as soon as its branch becomes tender and puts forth its leaves, you know that summer is near. So also, when you see all these things, you know that he is near, at the very gates. Truly, I say to you, this generation will not pass away till all these things take place. Heaven and earth will pass away, but my words will not pass away.

But of that day and hour no one knows, not even the angels of heaven, nor the Son, but the Father only. As were the days of Noah, so will be the coming of the Son of man. For as in those days before the flood they were eating and drinking, marrying and giving in marriage, until the day when Noah entered the ark, and they did not know until the flood came and swept them all away, so will be the coming of the Son of man. Then two men will be in the field; one is taken and one is left. Two women will be grinding at the mill; one is taken and one is left. Watch therefore, for you do not know on what day your Lord is coming. But know this, that if the householder had known in what part of the night the thief was coming, he would have watched and would not have let his house be broken into. Therefore you also must be ready; for the Son of man is coming at an hour you do not expect.

Who then is the faithful and wise servant, whom his master has set over his household, to give them their food at the proper time? Blessed is that servant whom his master when he comes will find so doing. Truly, I say to you, he will set him over all his possessions. But if that wicked servant says to himself, "My master is delayed," and begins to beat his fellow servants, and eats and drinks with the drunken, the master of that servant will come on a day when he does not expect him and at an hour he does not know, and will punish him, and put him with the hypocrites; there men will weep and gnash their teeth.

Matt. 24:4-51

. . . Woe to you, Chorazin! woe to you, Bethsaida! for if the mighty works done in you had been done in Tyre and Sidon, they would have repented long ago in sackcloth and ashes. But I tell you, it shall be more tolerable on the day of judgment for Tyre and Sidon than for you. And you, Capernaum, will you be exalted to heaven? You shall be brought down to Hades. For if the mighty works done in you had been done in Sodom, it would have remained until this day. But I tell you that it shall be more tolerable on the day of judgment for the land of Sodom than for you.

Matt. 11:21-24

. . . Do you see these great buildings? There will not be left here one stone upon another, that will not be thrown down.

. . . Take heed that no one leads you astray. Many will come in my name, saying, "I am he!" and they will lead many astray. And when you hear of wars and rumors of wars, do not be alarmed; this must take place, but the end is not yet. For nation will rise against nation, and kingdom against kingdom; there will be earthquakes in various places, there will be famines; this is but the beginning of the sufferings.

But take heed to yourselves; for they will deliver you up to councils; and you will be beaten in synagogues; and you will stand before governors and kings for my sake, to bear testimony before them. And the gospel must first be preached to all nations. And when they bring you to trial and deliver you up, do not be anxious beforehand what you are to say; but say whatever is given you in that hour, for it is not you who speak, but the Holy Spirit. And brother **Holy Spirit** will deliver up brother to death, and the father his child, and children will rise against parents and have them put to death; and you will be hated by all for my name's sake. But he who endures to the end will be saved.

Mark 13:2-13

. . . As for these things which you see, the days will come when there shall not be left here one stone upon another that will not be thrown down. . . . Take heed that you are not led astray; for many will come in my name, saying, "I am he!" and, "The time is at hand!" Do not go after them. And when you hear of wars and tumults, do not be terrified; for this must first take place, but the end will not be at once.

. . . Nation will rise against nation, and kingdom against kingdom; there will be great earthquakes, and in various places famines and pestilences; and there will be terrors and great signs from heaven. But before all this they will lay their hands on you and persecute you, delivering you up to the synagogues and prisons, and you will be brought before kings and governors for my name's sake. This will be a time for you to bear testimony. Settle it therefore in your minds, not to meditate beforehand how to answer; for I will give you a mouth and wisdom, which none of your adversaries will be able to withstand or contradict. You will be delivered up even by parents and brothers and kinsmen and friends, and some of you they will put to death; you will be hated by all for my name's sake. But not a hair of your head will perish. By your endurance you will gain your lives.

Luke 21:5-19

But when you see the desolating sacrilege set up where it ought not to be (let the reader understand), then let those who are in Judea flee to the mountains;

let him who is on the housetop not go down, nor enter his house, to take anything away; and let him who is in the field not turn back to take his mantle. And alas for those who are with child and for those who give suck in those days! Pray that it may not happen in winter. For in those days there will be such tribulation as has not been from the beginning of the creation which God created until now, and never will be. And if the Lord had not shortened the days, no human being would be saved; but for the sake of the elect, whom he chose, he shortened the days. And then if any one says to you, "Look, here is the Christ!" or "Look, there he is!" do not believe it. False Christs and false prophets will arise and show signs and wonders, to lead astray, if possible, the elect. But take heed; I have told you all things beforehand.

But in those days, after that tribulation, the sun will be darkened, and the moon will not give its light, and the stars will be falling from heaven, and the powers in the heavens will be shaken. And then they will see the Son of man coming in clouds with "second coming" great power and glory. And then he will send out the angels, and gather his elect from the four winds, from the ends of the earth to the ends of heaven.

From the fig tree learn its lesson: as soon as its branch becomes tender and puts forth its leaves, you know that summer is near. So also, when you see these things taking place, you know that he is near, at the very gates. Truly, I say to you, this generation will not pass away before all these things take place. Heaven and earth will pass away, but my words will not pass away.

But of that day or that hour no one knows, not even the angels in heaven, nor the Son, but only the Father. Take heed, watch; for you do not know when the time will come. It is like a man going on a journey, when he leaves home and puts his prayer servants in charge, each with his work, and commands the doorkeeper to be on the watch. Watch therefore— for you do not know when the master of the house will come, in the evening, or at midnight, or at cockcrow, or in the morning—lest he come suddenly and find you asleep. And what I say to you I say to all: Watch.

Mark 13:14-37

But when you see Jerusalem surrounded by armies, then know that its desolation has come near. Then let those who are in Judea flee to the mountains, and let those who are inside the city depart, and let not those who are out in the country enter it; for these are days of vengeance, to fulfil all that is written. Alas for those who are with child and for those who give suck in those days! For great distress shall be upon the earth and wrath upon this people; they will fall by the edge of the sword, and be led captive among all nations; and Jerusalem will be trodden down by the Gentiles, until the times of the Gentiles are fulfilled.

And there will be signs in sun and moon and stars, and upon the earth distress of nations in perplexity at the roaring of the sea and the waves, men fainting with fear and with foreboding of what is coming on the world; for the powers of the heavens will be shaken. And then they will see the Son of "second coming" man coming in a cloud with power and great glory. Now when these things begin to take place, look up and raise your heads, because your redemption is drawing near.

. . . Look at the fig tree, and all the trees; as soon as they come out in leaf, you see for yourselves and know that the summer is already near. So also, when you see these things taking kingdom of place, you know that the kingdom of God God is near. Truly, I say to you, this generation will not pass away till all has taken place. Heaven and earth will pass away, but my words will not pass away.

But take heed to yourselves lest your hearts be weighed down with dissipation and drunkenness and cares of this life, and that day come up- on you suddenly like a snare; for it will drunkenness come upon all who dwell upon the face of the whole earth. But watch at all times, praying that you may have strength to escape all these things that will take place, and to stand before the Son of man.

Luke 21:20-36

When the Son of man comes in his glory, and all the angels with him, then he will sit on his glorious throne. Before him will be gathered all the nations, and he will separate them one from another as a shepherd separates the sheep from the goats, and he will place the sheep at his right hand, but the goats at the left. Then the King will say to those at his right hand, "Come, O blessed of my Father, inherit the kingdom prepared for you from the foundation of the world; for I was hungry and you gave me food, I was thirsty and you gave me drink, I was a stranger and you welcomed me, I was naked and you clothed me, I was sick and you visited me, I was in prison and you came to me." Then the righteous will answer him, "Lord, when did we see thee hungry and feed thee, or thirsty and give thee drink? And when did we see thee a stranger and welcome thee, or naked and clothe thee? And when did we see thee sick or in prison and visit thee?" And the King will answer them, "Truly, I say to you, as you did it to one of the least of these my brethren, you **brotherhood** did it to me." Then he will say to those at his left hand, "Depart from me, you cursed, into the eternal fire prepared for the devil and his angels; for I was hungry and you gave me no food, I was thirsty and you gave me no drink, I was a stranger and you did not welcome me, naked and you did not clothe me, sick and in prison and you did not visit me." Then they also will answer, "Lord, when did we see thee hungry or thirsty or a stranger or naked or sick or in prison, and did not minister to thee?" Then he will answer them, "Truly, I say to you, as you did it not to one of the least of these, you did it not to me." And **eternal life** they will go away into eternal punishment, but the righteous into eternal life.

Matt. 25:31-46

. . . Daughters of Jerusalem, do not weep for me, but weep for yourselves, and for your children. For behold, the days are coming when they will say, "Blessed are the barren, and the wombs that never bore, and the breasts that never gave suck!" Then they will begin to say to the mountains, "Fall on us"; and to the hills, "Cover us." For if they do this when the wood is green, what will happen when it is dry?

Luke 23:28-31

. . . I have not a demon; but I honor my Father, and you dishonor me. Yet I do not seek my own glory; there is One who seeks it and he will be the judge. Truly, truly, I say to you, if any one keeps my word, he will never see death. **death**

John 8:49-51

. . . He who believes in me, believes not in me but in him who sent me. And he who sees me sees him who sent me. I have come as light into the world, that whoever believes in me may not remain in darkness. If any one hears my sayings and does not keep them, I do not judge him for I did not come to judge the world but to save the world. He who rejects me and does not receive my sayings has a judge; the word that I have spoken will be his judge on the last day. For I have not spoken on my own authority; the Father who sent me has himself given me commandment what to say and what to speak. And I know that his commandment is eternal life. What I say, therefore, I say as the Father has bidden me. **faith** **life**

John 12:44-50

I am the Alpha and the Omega. . . .
. . . Write what you see in a book and send it to the seven churches, to Ephesus and to Smyrna and to Pergamum and to Thyatira and to Sardis and to Philadelphia and to Laodicea.
. . . Fear not, I am the first and the last; and the living

one; I died, and behold I am alive for evermore, and I have the keys of Death and Hades. Now write what you see, what is and what is to take place hereafter. As for the mystery of the seven stars which you saw in my right hand, and the seven golden lampstands, the seven stars are the angels of the seven churches and the seven lampstands are the seven churches.

To the angel of the church in Ephesus write: "The words of him who holds the seven stars in his right hand, who walks among the seven golden lampstands.

"I know your works, your toil and your patient endurance, and how you cannot bear evil men but have tested those who call themselves apostles but are not and found them to be false; I know you are enduring patiently and bearing up for my name's sake, and you have not grown weary. But I have this against you, that you have abandoned the love you had at first. Remember then from what you have fallen, repent and do the works you did at first. If not, I will come to you and remove your lampstand from its place, unless you repent. Yet this you have, you hate the works of the Nicolaitans, which I also hate. He who has an ear, let him hear what the Spirit says to the churches. To him who conquers I will grant to eat of the tree of life, which is in the paradise of God."

And to the angel of the church in Smyrna write: "The words of the first and the last, who died and came to life.

"I know your tribulation and your poverty (but you are rich) and the slander of those who say that they are Jews and are not, but are a synagogue of Satan. Do not fear what you are about to suffer. Behold, the devil is about to throw some of you into prison, that you may be tested, and for ten days you will have tribulation. Be faithful unto death, and I will give you the crown of life. He who has an ear, let him hear what the Spirit says to the churches. He who conquers shall not be hurt by the second death."

And to the angel of the church in Pergamum write: "The words of him who has the sharp two-edged sword.

"I know where you dwell, where Satan's throne is; you hold fast my name and you did not deny my faith even in the days of Antipas my witness, my faithful one, who was killed among you, where Satan dwells. But I have a few things against you: you have some there who hold the teaching of Balaam, who taught Balak to put a stumbling block before the sons of Israel, that they might eat food sacrificed to idols and practice immorality. So you also have some who hold the teaching of the Nicolaitans. Repent then. If not, I will come to you soon and   **repentance** war against them with the sword of my mouth. He who has an ear, let him hear what the Spirit says to the churches. To him who conquers I will give some of the hidden manna, and I will give him a white stone, with a new name written on the stone which no one knows except him who receives it."

And to the angel of the church in Thyatira write: "The words of the Son of God, who has eyes like a flame of fire, and whose feet are like burnished bronze.

"I know your works, your love and faith and service and patient endurance, and that your latter works exceed the first. But I have this against you, that you tolerate the woman Jezebel, who calls herself a prophetess and is teaching and beguiling my servants to practice immorality and to eat food sacrificed to idols. I gave her time to repent, but she refuses to repent of her immorality. Behold, I will throw her on a sickbed, and those who commit adultery with her   **sin** I will throw into great tribulation, unless they repent of her doings; and I will strike her children dead. And all the churches shall know that I am he who searches mind and heart, and I will give to each of you as your works deserve. But to the rest of you in Thyatira, who do not hold this teaching, who have not learned what some call the deep things of Satan, to you I say,

I do not lay upon you any other burden; only hold fast what you have, until I come. He who conquers and who keeps my works until the end, I will give him power over the nations, and he shall rule them with a rod of iron, as when earthen pots are broken in pieces, even as I myself have received power from my Father; and I will give him the morning star. He who has an ear, let him hear what the Spirit says to the churches."

And to the angel of the church in Sardis write: "The words of him who has the seven spirits of God and the seven stars.

"I know your works; you have the name of being alive, and you are dead. Awake, and strengthen what remains and is on the point of death, for I have not found your works perfect in the sight of my God. Remember then what you received and heard; keep that, and repent. If you will not awake, I will come like a thief, and you will not know at what hour I will come upon you. Yet you have still a few names in Sardis, people who have not soiled their garments; and they shall walk with me in white, for they are worthy. He who conquers shall be clad thus in white garments, and I will not blot his name out of the book of life; I will confess his name be- **reward** fore my Father and before his angels. He who has an ear, let him hear what the Spirit says to the churches."

And to the angel of the church in Philadelphia write: "The words of the holy one, the true one, who has the key of David, who opens and no one shall shut, who shuts and no one opens.

"I know your works. Behold, I have set before you an open door, which no one is able to shut; I know that you have but little power, and yet you have kept my word and have not denied my name. Behold, I will make those of the synagogue of Satan who say that they are Jews and are not, but lie—behold, I will make them come and bow down before your feet, and learn that I have loved you. Because you have kept my word of patient endurance, I will keep you from the hour of trial which is coming on the whole world, to try those who dwell upon the earth. I am coming soon; hold fast what you have, so that no one may seize your crown. He who conquers, I will make him a pillar in the temple of my God; never shall he go out of it, and I will write on him the name of my God, and the name of the city of my God, the New Jerusalem which comes down from my God out of heaven, and my own new name. He who has an ear, let him hear what the Spirit says to the churches."

And to the angel of the church in Laodicea write: "The words of the Amen, the faithful and true witness, the beginning of God's creation.

"I know your works: you are neither cold nor hot. Would that you were cold or hot! So, because you are lukewarm, and neither cold nor hot, I will spew you out of my mouth. For you say, I am rich, I have prospered, and I need nothing; not knowing **money** that you are wretched, pitiable, poor, blind and naked. Therefore I counsel you to buy from me gold refined by fire, that you may be rich, and white garments to clothe you and to keep the shame of your nakedness from being seen, and salve to anoint your eyes, that you may see. Those whom I love, I reprove and chasten; so be zealous and repent. Behold, I stand at the door and knock; if any one hears my voice and opens the door, I will come in to him and eat with him, and he with me. He who conquers I **evangelism** will grant him to sit with me on my throne, as I myself conquered and sat down with my Father on his throne. He who has an ear, let him hear **reward** what the Spirit says to the churches."

Rev. 1:8-3, 22

... And behold, I am coming soon.
... You must not do that! I am a fellow servant with you and your brethren the prophets, and with those who keep the words of this book. Worship God.
    ... Do not seal up the words of the prophecy of this

book, for the time is near. Let the evildoer still do evil, and the filthy still be filthy, and the righteous still do right, and the holy still be holy.

Behold, I am coming soon, bringing my recompense, to repay every one for what he has done. I am the Alpha and the Omega, the first and the last, the beginning and the end.

I Jesus have sent my angel to you with this testimony for the churches. I am the root and the offspring of David, the bright morning star.

Rev. 22:7-16

Kingdom of Heaven

One of the greatest concepts given by the Jewish faith to Western culture is that God is the ruler of all life. This was the structure of relationship between God and man as viewed by the Jews. He is the king and we are his subjects. Jesus accepted and used this analogy to carry his message of good news to the people.

Sometimes the divine rule is called "kingdom of God" as in Mark and Luke, at other times it is called the "kingdom of heaven" as in Matthew. When and how the kingdom was coming could not be known precisely. Different Jews had different answers, but they agreed that an ideal rule of God over all creation was coming.

Thus, when Jesus began his ministry with the words, "the kingdom of heaven is at hand," his startled listeners tuned their ears to his attention. This was certainly good news, for it meant to the people that God was at last ready to begin his reign. As time went on, the crowds became less and less enthusiastic because they learned that the kingdom set an obligation upon them—obedience to God.

Jesus' ministry soon revealed that many of those who talked about the kingdom were really unwilling for

113

God to rule—they were unwilling to make the changes in their lives that would let God rule.

One of Jesus' tasks was to help his people understand the true nature of the kingdom. It was God's rule over the community, the nation. Yet this rule must begin in the heart: "behold the kingdom of God is in the midst of you."

* * *

... Repent, for the kingdom of heaven is at hand.   **repentance**

Matt. 4:17

... The time is fulfilled, and the kingdom of God is at hand; repent, and believe in the gospel.

Mark 1:15

... Whoever then relaxes one of the least of these commandments and teaches men so, shall be called least in the kingdom of heaven; but he who does them and teaches them shall be called great in the kingdom of heaven. For I tell you, unless your righteousness exceeds that of the scribes and Pharisees, you will never enter the kingdom of heaven.

Matt. 5:19-20

... The kingdom of heaven may be compared to a man who sowed good seed in his field; but while men were sleeping, his enemy came and sowed weeds among the wheat, and went away. So when the plants came up and bore grain, then the weeds appeared also. And the servants of the householder came and said to him, "Sir, did you not sow good seed in your field? How then has it weeds?" He said to them, "An enemy has done this." The servants said to him, "Then do you want us to go and gather them?" But he said, "No; lest in gathering the weeds you root up the wheat along with them. Let both grow together until the harvest; and at harvest time I will tell   **judgment** the reapers, Gather the weeds first and bind them in bundles to be burned, but gather the wheat into my barn."

Matt. 13:24-30

. . . The kingdom of heaven is like a grain of mustard seed which a man took and sowed in his field; it is the smallest of all seeds, but when it has grown it is the greatest of shrubs and becomes a tree, so that the birds of the air come and make nests in its branches.

Matt. 13:24-32

. . . He who sows the good seed is the Son of man; the field is the world, and the good seed means the sons of the kingdom; the weeds are the sons of the evil one, and the enemy who sowed them is the devil; the harvest is the close of the age, and the reapers are angels. Just as the weeds are gathered and burned with fire, so will it be at the close of the age. The Son of man will send his angels, and they will gather out of his kingdom all causes of sin and all evildoers, and throw them into the furnace of fire; there men will weep and gnash their teeth. Then the righteous will shine like the sun in the kingdom of their Father. He who has ears, let him hear.

Matt. 13:37-43

. . . It is like a grain of mustard seed, which, when sown upon the ground, is the smallest of all the seeds on earth; yet when it is sown it grows up and becomes the greatest of all shrubs, and puts forth large branches, so that the birds of the air can make nests in its shade.

Mark 4:31-32

. . . What is the kingdom of God like? And to what shall I compare it? It is like a grain of mustard seed which a man took and sowed in his garden; and it grew and became a tree, and the birds of the air made nests in its branches.

Luke 13:18-19

. . . The kingdom of heaven is like leaven which a woman took and hid in three measures of meal, till it was all leavened.

Matt. 13:33

. . . To what shall I compare the kingdom of God? It is like leaven which a woman took and hid in three measures of meal, till it was all leavened.

Luke 13:20-21

The kingdom of heaven is like treasure hidden in a field, which a man found and covered up; then in his joy he goes and sells all that he has and buys that field.

Again, the kingdom of heaven is like a merchant in search of fine pearls, who, on finding one pearl of great value, went and sold all that he had and bought it.

Again, the kingdom of heaven is like a net which was thrown into the sea and gathered fish of every kind; when it was full, men drew it ashore and sat down and sorted the good into vessels but threw away the bad. So it will be at the **judgment** close of the age. The angels will come out and separate the evil from the righteous, and throw them into the furnace of fire; there men will weep and gnash their teeth.

Have you understood all this? . . . Therefore every scribe who has been trained for the kingdom of heaven is like a householder who brings out of his treasure what is new and what is old.

Matt. 13:44-52

. . . Truly, I say to you, unless you turn and become like children, you will never enter the kingdom of heaven. Whoever humbles himself **children** like this child, he is the greatest in the kingdom of heaven.

Whoever receives one such child in my name receives me; but whoever causes one of these little ones who believe in me to sin, it would be better for him to have a great millstone fastened round **judgment** his neck and to be drowned in the depth of the sea.

Matt. 18:3-6

. . . Let the children come to me, and do not hinder them; for to such belongs the king- **children** dom of heaven.

Matt. 19:14

For the kingdom of heaven is like a householder who went out early in the morning to hire laborers for his vineyard. After agreeing with the laborers for a denarius a day, he sent them into his vineyard. And going out about the third hour he saw others standing idle in the market place; and to them he said, "You go into the vineyard too, and whatever is right I will give you." So they went. Going out again about the sixth hour and the ninth hour, he did the same. And about the eleventh hour he went out and found others standing; and he said to them, "Why do you stand here idle all day?" They said to him, "Because no one has hired us." He said to them, "You go into the vineyard too." And when evening came, the owner of the vineyard said to his steward, "Call the laborers and pay them their wages, beginning with the last, up to the first." And when those hired about the eleventh hour came, each of them received a denarius. Now when the first came, they thought they would receive more; but each of them also received a **rewards** denarius. And on receiving it they grumbled at the householder, saying, "These last worked only one hour, and you have made them equal to us who have borne the burden of the day and the scorching heat." But he replied to one of them, "Friend, I am doing you no wrong; did you not agree with me for a denarius? Take what belongs to you, and go; I choose to give to this last as I give to you. Am I not allowed to do what I choose with what belongs to me? Or do you begrudge my generosity?" So the last will be first, and the first last.

Matt. 20:1-16

. . . The kingdom of heaven may be compared to a king who gave a marriage feast for his son, and sent his servants to call those who were invited to the marriage feast; but they would not come. Again he sent other servants, saying, "Tell those who are invited, Behold, I have made ready my dinner, my oxen and my fat calves are killed, and everything is ready; come to the marriage feast." But they made light of it and went off, one to his farm, another to his business, while the rest seized his servants, treated them shamefully, and killed them. The king was angry, and he sent his troops and destroyed those murderers and burned their city. Then he said to his servants, "The wedding is ready, but those invited were not worthy. Go therefore to the thoroughfares, and invite to the marriage feast as many as you find." And those servants went out into the streets and gathered all whom they found, both bad and good; so the wedding hall was filled with guests.

But when the king came in to look at the guests, he saw there a man who had no wedding garment; and he said to him, "Friend, how did you get in here without a wedding garment?" And he was speechless. Then the king said to the attendants, "Bind him hand and foot, and cast him into the outer darkness; there men will weep and gnash their teeth." For many are called, but few are chosen.

Matt. 22:2-14

. . . A man once gave a great banquet, and invited many; and at the time for the banquet he sent his servant to say to those who had been invited, "Come; for all is now ready." But they all alike began to make excuses. The first said to him, "I have bought a field, and I must go out and see it; I pray you, have me excused." And another said, "I have bought five yoke of oxen, and I go to examine them; I pray you, have me excused." And another said, "I have married a wife, and therefore I cannot come." So the servant came and reported this to his master. Then the householder in anger said to his servant, "Go out quickly to the streets and lanes of the city, and bring in the poor and maimed and blind and lame." And the servant said, "Sir, what you commanded has been done, and still there is room." And the master said to the servant, "Go out to the highways and hedges, and compel people to come in, that my house may be filled. For I tell you, none of those men who were invited shall taste my banquet."

Luke 14:16-24

. . . The kingdom of God is not coming with signs to be observed; nor will they say, "Lo, here it is!" or "There!" for behold, the kingdom of God is in the midst of you.

Luke 17:20-21

. . . Let the children come to me, and do not hinder them; for to such belongs the kingdom of God. Truly, I say to you, whoever does not **children** receive the kingdom of God like a child shall not enter it.

Luke 18:16-17

Then the kingdom of heaven shall be compared to ten maidens who took their lamps and went to meet the bridegroom. Five of them were foolish, and five were wise. For when the foolish took their lamps, they took no oil with them; but the wise took flasks of oil with their lamps. As the bridegroom was delayed, they all slumbered and slept. But at midnight there was a cry, "Behold, the bridegroom! Come out to meet him." Then all those maidens rose and trimmed their lamps. And the foolish said to the wise, "Give us some of your oil, for our lamps are going out." But the wise replied, "Perhaps there will not be enough for us and for you; go rather to the dealers and buy for yourselves." And while they went to buy, the bridegroom came, and those who were ready went in with him to the marriage feast; and the door was shut. Afterward the other maidens came also, saying, "Lord, lord, open to us." But he replied, "Truly, I say to you, I do not know you." Watch therefore, for you know neither the day nor the hour.

For it will be as when a man going on a journey called his servants and entrusted to them his property; to one he gave five talents, to another two, to another one, to each according to his ability. Then he went away. He who had received the five talents went at once and traded with them; and he made five talents more. So too, he who had the two talents made two talents more. But he who had received the one talent went and dug in the ground and hid his master's money. Now after a long time the master of those servants came and settled accounts with them. And he who had received the five talents came forward, bringing five talents more, saying, "Master, you delivered to me five talents; here I have made five talents more." His master said to him, "Well done, good and faithful servant; you have been faithful over a little, I will set you over much; enter into the joy of your master." And he also who had the two talents came forward, saying, "Master, you delivered to me two talents; here I have made two talents more." His master said to him, "Well done, good and faithful servant; you have been faithful over a little, I will set you over much; enter into the joy of your master." He also who had received the one talent came forward, saying, "Master, I knew you to be a hard man, reaping where you did not sow, and gathering where you did not winnow; so I was afraid, and I went and hid your talent in the ground. Here you have what is yours." But his master answered him, "You wicked and slothful servant! You knew that I reap where I have not sowed, and gather where I have not winnowed? Then you ought to have invested my money with the bankers, and at my coming I should have received what was my own with interest. So take the talent from him, and give it to him who has the ten talents. For to every one who has will more be given, and he will have abundance; but from him who has not, even what he has will be taken away. And cast the worthless servant into the outer darkness; there men will weep and gnash their teeth."

Matt. 25:1-30

Let not your hearts be troubled; believe in God, believe also in me. In my Father's house are many rooms; if it were not so, would I have told **heaven** you that I go to prepare a place for you? And when I go and prepare a place for you, I will come again and will take you to myself, that where I am you may be also. And you know the way where I am going.

John 14:1-4

Love—Brotherhood

(HUMAN RELATIONS)

No other quality of God is so easily seen in the life and teachings of Jesus as the quality of love. Indeed, love is so central to the character of God, as presented in and by Jesus, that some of the New Testament writers say God *is* Love.

Love is a broad term, with many levels of intensity and purity, but certainly divine love is the highest of all. Human love may approach divine love, however, and Jesus urged his followers to participate in the divine love in their relationships with each other.

The love of Jesus is not a sentimental, romantic love, the kind of "love" which permeates American culture until it becomes an idol of worship for advertisers and filmmakers. The love of Jesus is a hard-headed, down-to-earth real love for those considered unlovely as well as the lovely in our society. It is love that encourages the depressed and weary, and wants justice and forgiveness, and a better life for the downtrodden. This love is tough; it has to be to remain love, and not degenerate into despair or cynicism.

The two greatest commandments, Jesus pointed out, are those demanding the love of God and love of one's

123

neighbor. And he made it clear in his story of the Good Samaritan that neighbor means *anyone in need*.

The whole man given in love was Jesus' ideal of goodness. This goodness, essential to God's kingdom, is a light shining from within and reflecting outward through one's behavior, through his acts toward God, himself, and other people.

This love is the key to our survival on earth and salvation in heaven.

* * *

You have heard that it was said to the men of old, "You shall not kill; and whoever kills shall be liable to judgment." But I say to you that every one who is angry with his brother shall be liable to judgment; whoever insults his brother shall be liable to the council, and whoever says, "You fool!" shall be liable to the hell of fire. So if you are offering **hell** your gift at the altar, and there remember that your brother has something against you, leave your gift there before the altar and go; first be reconciled to your brother, and then come and offer your gift. Make friends quickly with your accuser, while you are going with him to court, lest your accuser hand you over to the judge, and the judge to the guard, and you be put in prison; truly, I say to you, you will never get out till you have paid the last penny.

Matt. 5:21-26

You have heard that it was said, "An eye for an eye and a tooth for a tooth." But I say to you, Do not resist one who is evil. But if any one strikes you on the right cheek, turn to him the other also; and if any one would sue you and take your coat, let him have your cloak as well; and if any one forces you to go one mile, go with him two miles.

Matt. 5:38-41

You have heard that it was said, "You shall love your neighbor and hate your enemy." But I say to you, Love your enemies and pray for those who persecute you, so that you may be sons of your Father who is in heaven; for he makes his sun rise on the evil and on the good, and sends rain on the just and on the unjust. For if you love those who love you, what reward have you? Do not even the tax collectors do the same? And if you salute only your brethren, what more are you doing than others? Do not even the Gentiles do the same? You, therefore, must be perfect, as your heavenly Father is perfect.

Matt. 5:43-48

But I say to you that hear, Love your enemies, do good to those who hate you, bless those who curse you, pray for those who abuse you. To him who strikes you on the cheek, offer the other also; and from him who takes away your cloak do not withhold your coat as well. Give to every one who begs from you; and of him who takes away your goods, do not ask them again. And as you wish that men would do to you, do so to them.

If you love those who love you, what credit is that to you? For even sinners love those who love them. And if you do good to those who do good to you, what credit is that to you? For even sinners do the same. And if you lend to those from whom you hope to receive, what credit is that to you? Even sinners lend to sinners, to receive as much again. But love your enemies, and do good, and lend, expecting nothing in return; and your reward will be great, and you will be sons of the Most High; for he is kind to the ungrateful and the selfish. Be merciful, even as your Father is merciful.

Luke 6:27-36

Judge not, that you be not judged. For with the judgment you pronounce you will be judged, and the measure you give will be **judgment** the measure you get.

Matt. 7:1-2

Judge not, and you will not be judged; condemn not, and you will not be condemned; forgive, and you will be forgiven; give, and **forgiveness** it will be given to you; good measure, pressed down, shaken together, running over, will be put into your lap. For the measure you give will be the **giving** measure you get back.

Luke 6:37-38

. . . So whatever you wish that men would do to you, do so to them; for this is the law and the prophets.

Matt. 7:12

. . . Who is my mother, and who are my brothers? . . . Here are my mother and my brothers! For whoever does the will of my Father in heaven is my brother, and sister, and mother.

Matt. 12:48-50

. . . Who are my mother and my brothers? . . . Here are my mother and my brother! Whoever does the will of God is my brother, and sister, and mother.

Mark 3:33-35

. . . My mother and my brothers are those who hear the word of God and do it.

Luke 8:21

If your brother sins against you, go and tell him his fault, between you and him alone. If he listens to you, you have gained your brother. But if he does not listen, take one or two others along with you, that every word may be confirmed by the evidence of two or three witnesses. If he refuses to listen to them, tell it to the church; and if he refuses to listen even to the church, let him be to you as a Gentile and a tax collector.

Matt. 18:15-17

. . . What is written in the law? How do you read? . . . You have answered right; do this, and you will live.

. . . A man was going down from Jerusalem to Jericho, and he fell among robbers, who stripped him and beat him, and departed, leaving him half dead. Now by chance a priest was going down that road; and when he saw him he passed by on the other side. So likewise a Levite, when he came to the place and saw him, passed by on the other side. But a Samaritan, as he journeyed, came to where he was; and when he saw him, he had compassion, and went to him and bound up his wounds, pouring on oil and wine; then he set him on his own beast and brought him to an inn, and took care of him. And the next day he took out two denarii and gave them to the innkeeper, saying, "Take care of him; and whatever more you spend, I will repay you when I come back." Which of these three, do you think, proved neighbor to the man who fell among the robbers? . . . Go and do likewise.

Luke 10:26-37

. . . As you go with your accuser before the magistrate, make an effort to settle with him on the way, lest he drag you to the judge, and the judge hand you over to the officer, and the officer put you in prison. I tell you, you will never get out till you have paid the very last copper. **judgment**

Luke 12:58-59

. . . What do you want? . . . You do not know what you are asking. Are you able to drink the cup that I am to drink? . . . You will drink my cup, but to sit at my right hand and at my left is not mine to grant, but it is for those for whom it has been prepared by my Father. . . . You know that the rulers of the Gentiles lord it over them, and their great men exercise authority over them. It shall not be so among you; but whoever would be great among you must be your servant, and whoever would be first **humility** among you must be your slave. . . .

Matt. 20:21-27

. . . What do you want me to do for you? . . . You do not know what you are asking. Are you able to drink the cup that I drink, or to be baptized with the baptism with which I am baptized? . . . The cup that I drink you will drink; and with the baptism with which I am baptized, you will be baptized; but to sit at my right hand or at my left is not mine to grant, but it is for those for whom it has been prepared. . . . You know that those who are supposed to rule over the Gentiles lord it over them, and their great men exercise authority over them. But it shall not be so among you; but whoever would be great among you must be your servant, and whoever would be first among you must be slave of all.

Mark 10:36-44

. . . You shall love the Lord your God with all your heart, and with all your soul, and with all your mind. This is the great and first commandment. And a second is like it, You shall love your neighbor as yourself. On these two commandments depend all the law and the prophets.

Matt. 22:37-40

. . . The first is, "Hear, O Israel: The Lord our God, the Lord is one; and you shall love the Lord your God with all your heart, and with all your soul, and with all your mind, and with all your strength." The second is this, "You shall love your neighbor as yourself." There is no other commandment greater than these.

Mark 12:29-31

. . . Little children, yet a little while I am with you. You will seek me; and as I said to the Jews so now I say to you, "Where I am going you cannot come." A new commandment I give to you, that you love one another; even as I have loved you, that you also love one another. By this all men will know that you are my disciples, if you have love for one another.

John 13:33-35

. . . Peace I leave with you; my peace I give to you; not as the world gives do I give to you. Let not your hearts be troubled, neither let them be afraid. You heard me say to you, "I go away, and I **peace** will come to you." If you loved me, you would have rejoiced, because I go to the Father; for the Father is greater than I. And now I have told you before it takes place, so that when it does take place, **God** you may believe. I will no longer talk much with you, for the ruler of this world is coming. He has no power over me; but I do as the Father has commanded me, so that the world may know that I love the Father. Rise, let us go hence.

John 14:27-31

. . . As the Father has loved me, so have I loved you; abide in my love. If you keep my commandments, you will abide in my love, just as I have kept my Father's commandments and abide in his love. These things I have spoken to you, that my joy may be in you, and that your joy may be full.

This is my commandment, that you love one another as I have loved you. Greater love has no man than this, that a man lay down his life for his friends. You are my friends if you do what I command you. No longer do I call you servants, for the servant does not know what his master is doing; but I have called you friends, for all that I have heard from my Father I have made known to you. You did not choose me, but I chose you and appointed you that you should go and bear fruit and that your fruit should abide; so that whatever you ask the Father in my name, he may give it to you. This I command you, to love one another.

John 15:9-17

I do not pray for these only, but also for those who believe in me through their word, that they may all be one; even as thou, Father, art in me, and I in thee, that they also may be in us, so that the world may

believe that thou hast sent me. The glory which thou
hast given me I have given to them, that they may be
one even as we are one, I in them and thou in me,
that they may become perfectly one, so that the world
may know that thou hast sent me and hast loved them
even as thou hast loved me. Father, I desire that they
also, whom thou hast given me, may be with me where
I am, to behold my glory which thou hast given me
in thy love for me before the foundation of the world.
O righteous Father, the world has not known thee,
but I have known thee; and these know that thou
hast sent me. I made known to them thy name, and I
will make it known, that the love with which thou hast
loved me may be in them, and I in them.

John 17:20-26

Marriage—Divorce

Jesus' teaching about marriage has sometimes been discredited by his critics because he never married. "How could he know?" is their cry as they compare his teaching to their own experience. They do not credit Jesus' understanding of marriage that he gained through his experience of the closely-knit Jewish family life of which he was an important part.

Most scholars believe that Joseph died while Jesus was in his teens. As the oldest child, Jesus would have been responsible for working in the carpenter shop to support his mother, brothers and sisters until his brothers were able to take over this responsibility. Coffee and Cowen's provocative play, *Family Portrait,* gives us a delightful, if fictional, account of what could very well have been the everyday life of Jesus' family.

The Jewish faith placed a high value on the life of the family, the fidelity of husband and wife, the loyalty of parents to children and children to parents. Out of this experience, and out of his thorough study of the Old Testament, Jesus developed his teachings on marriage.

Here we must call attention to a note in Jesus' thinking not found in the Old Testament. He said in effect that it is *not God's will* that any marriage end in divorce. Here, as in other areas of human behavior, Jesus held up before man the ideal of God's will.

His words against divorce have been difficult for many Christians to follow. But it was no easier in his own time. His own disciples said that if divorce is not permitted, it is better that a man should not marry!

Jesus' teaching on divorce changed the status of a woman in the marriage relationship from that of an inferior, subject to the whims of her husband, to her husband's equal. This was revolutionary in his day, and has ever since distinguished Christian culture from the other major cultures of the world.

Jesus does not answer all of our questions about the justice of specific divorces, but he is always interested in the best for an individual. He continues to love and care for those who are divorced.

Jesus was interested in persons and their freedom to grow spiritually. If his teachings on forgiveness and overcoming evil with good are applied to marriage, there should be less need for divorce. Jesus saw opportunity for spiritual growth in the family devoted to God.

* * *

It was also said, "Whoever divorces his wife, let him give her a certificate of divorce." But I say to you that every one who divorces his wife, except on the ground of unchastity, makes her an adulteress; and whoever marries a divorced woman commits adultery.

Matt. 5:31-32

. . . Have you not read that he who made them from the beginning made them male and female, and said, "For this reason a man shall leave his father and mother and be joined to his wife, and the two shall become one"? So they are no longer two but one. What therefore God has joined together, let no man put asunder. . . . For your hardness of heart Moses allowed you to divorce your wives, but from the beginning it was not so. And I say to you: whoever divorces his wife, except for unchastity, and marries another, commits adultery.

. . . Not all men can receive this precept, but only those to whom it is given. For there are eunuchs who have been so from birth, and there are eunuchs who have been made eunuchs by men, and there are eunuchs who have made themselves eunuchs for the sake of the kingdom of heaven. He who is able to receive this, let him receive it.

Matt. 19:4-12

. . . What did Moses command you? . . . . For your hardness of heart he wrote you this commandment. But from the beginning of creation, "God made them male and female." "For this reason a man shall leave his father and mother and be joined to his wife, and the two shall become one." So they are no longer two but one. What therefore God has joined together, let no man put asunder.

. . . Whoever divorces his wife and marries another, commits adultery against her; and if she divorces her husband and marries another, she commits adultery.

Mark 10:3-12

Every one who divorces his wife and marries another commits adultery, and he who marries a woman divorced from her husband commits adultery.

Luke 16:18

. . . You are wrong, because you know neither the scriptures nor the power of God. For in the resurrection they neither marry nor are given in marriage, but are like angels in heaven. And as for the resurrection of the dead, have you not read what was said to you by God, "I am the God of Abraham, and the God of Isaac, and the God of Jacob"? He is not God of the dead, but of the living.

Matt. 22:29-32

. . . Is not this why you are wrong, that you know neither the scriptures nor the power of God? For when they rise from the dead, they neither marry nor are given in marriage, but are like angels in heaven. And as for the dead being raised, have you not read in the book of Moses, in the passage about the bush, how God said to him, "I am the God of Abraham, and the God of Isaac, and the God of Jacob"? He is not God of the dead, but of the living; you are quite wrong.

Mark 12:24-27

. . . The sons of this age marry and are given in marriage; but those who are accounted worthy to attain to that age and to the resurrection from the dead neither marry nor are given in marriage, for they cannot die any more, because they are equal to angels and are sons of God, being sons of the resurrection. But that the dead are raised, even Moses showed, in the passage about the bush, where he calls the Lord the God of Abraham and the God of Isaac and the God of Jacob. Now he is not God of the dead, but of the living; for all live to him.

Luke 20:34-38

Money

(GIVING, WEALTH)

Jesus was acutely aware of the place of money in the lives of the people he taught. He pointed many of his words toward this subject and said some apparent contradictions. Thus, some readers of the Bible conclude that he condemned wealth; others feel he promised material rewards to his followers.

Each saying of Jesus on this subject should be studied in its context before drawing a final conclusion. For an adequate understanding of his teaching about money, we need to think back to his teaching about God and man's loyalty to him.

Jesus was not opposed to the private ownership of property nor to the normal process of making a living. He was opposed to a man's loyalty, devotion, and energy being devoted to and captivated by money, property, or wealth. To Jesus, there must be no pursuit as important as the pursuit of God's will. Every activity of life is to be subordinate to this. Fame, sex, making money, even the pursuit of art, culture, and wisdom, must not detract the person from his main goal of life. "You cannot serve God and mammon," Jesus said. Mammon is simply the Aramaic word for property.

Jesus saw danger in the pursuit of money not only because of what it might do to the individual, but what it might do to his relations with other men. How often do men gain money at the expense of others? Some desire money so strongly that they will sell anything, including themselves, for it. This lust for money Jesus condemned.

He said, "Do not be anxious about tomorrow." (This is a better translation of the original Greek than "Take no thought for the morrow." Matt. 6:34) Trust in our heavenly Father for every need should eliminate the anxiety we have about money. Work is necessary for our daily bread, but anxiety—never.

This requires faith deeper than most of us have, but Jesus invites us to follow him, to seek the kingdom first and "all these things shall be added to you."

* * *

... Give to him who begs from you, and do not refuse him who would borrow from you.

Matt. 5:42

Beware of practicing your piety before men in order to be seen by them; for then you will have no reward from your Father who is in heaven.

Thus, when you give alms, sound no trumpet before you, as the hypocrites do in the synagogues and in the streets, that they may be praised by men. Truly, I say to you, they have their reward. But when you give alms, do not let your left hand know reward what your right hand is doing, so that your alms may be in secret; and your Father who sees in secret will reward you.

Matt. 6:1-4

Do not lay up for yourselves treasures on earth, where moth and rust consume and where thieves break in and steal, but lay up for yourselves treasures in heaven, where neither moth nor rust consumes and where thieves do not break in and steal. For where your treasure is, there will your heart be also.

Matt. 6:19-21

. . . They need not go away; you give them something to eat. . . . Bring them here to me.

Matt. 14:16-18

. . . You give them something to eat. . . . How many loaves have you? Go and see.

Mark 6:37-38

. . . You give them something to eat. . . . Make them sit down in companies, about fifty each.

Luke 9:13-14

. . . How are we to buy bread, so that these people may eat? . . . Make the people sit down. . . . Gather up the fragments left over, that nothing may be lost.

John 6:5-12

. . . What do you think, Simon? From whom do kings of the earth take toll or tribute? From their sons or from others? . . . Then the sons are free. However, not to give offense to them, go to the sea and cast a hook, and take the first fish that comes up, and when you open its mouth you will find a shekel; take that and give it to them for me and for yourself.

Matt. 17:25-27

. . . Why put me to the test, you hypocrites? Show me the money for the tax. . . . Whose likeness and inscription is this? . . . Render therefore to Caesar the things that are Caesar's, and to God the things that are God's.

Matt. 22:18-21

. . . Why put me to the test? Bring me a coin, and let me look at it. . . . Whose likeness and inscription is this? . . . Render to Caesar the things that are Caesar's and to God the things that are God's.

Mark 12:15-17

. . . Show me a coin. Whose likeness and inscription has it? . . . Then render to Caesar the things that are Caesar's, and to God the things that are God's.

Luke 20:23-25

. . . Man, who made me a judge or divider over you? . . . Take heed, and beware of all covetousness; for a man's life does not consist in the abundance of his possessions. . . . The land of a rich man brought forth plentifully; and he thought to himself, "What shall I do, for I have nowhere to store my crops?" And he said, "I will do this: I will pull down my barns, and build larger ones; and there I will store all my grain and my goods. And I will say to my soul, Soul, you have ample goods laid up for many years; take your ease, eat, drink, be merry." But God said to him, "Fool! This night your soul is required of you; and the things you have prepared, whose will they be?" So is he who lays up treasure for himself, and is not rich toward God.

. . . Therefore I tell you, do not be anxious about your life, what you shall eat, nor about your body, what you shall put on. For life is more than food, and the body more than clothing. Consider the ravens: they neither sow nor reap, they have neither storehouse nor barn, and yet God feeds them. Of how much more value are you than the birds! And which of you by being anxious can add a cubit to his span of life? If then you are not able to do as small a thing as that, why are you anxious about the rest? Consider the lilies, how they grow; they neither toil nor spin; yet I tell you, even Solomon in all his glory was not arrayed like one of these. But if God so clothes the grass which is alive in the field today and tomorrow is thrown into the oven, how much more will he clothe you, O men of little faith! And do not seek what you are to eat and what you are to drink, nor be of anxious mind. For all the nations of the world seek these things; and your Father knows that you need them. Instead, seek his kingdom, and these things shall be yours as well.

Fear not, little flock, for it is your Father's good pleasure to give you the kingdom. Sell **kingdom of** your possessions, and give alms; provide **God** yourselves with purses that do not grow old, with a treasure in the heavens that does not fail, where no thief approaches and no moth destroys. For where your treasure is, there will your heart be also.

Luke 12:14-34

There was a rich man, who was clothed in purple and fine linen and who feasted sumptuously every day. And at his gate lay a poor man named Lazarus, full of sores, who desired to be fed with what fell from the rich man's table; moreover the dogs came and licked his sores. The poor man died and was carried by the angels to Abraham's bosom. The rich man also died and was buried; and in Hades, being in torment, he lifted up his eyes, and saw Abraham far off and Lazarus in his bosom. And he called out, "Father Abraham, have mercy upon me, and send Lazarus to dip the end of his finger in water and cool my tongue; for I am in anguish in this flame." But Abraham said, "Son, remember that you in your lifetime received your good things, and Lazarus in like manner evil things; but now he is comforted here, and you are in anguish. And besides all this, between us and you a great chasm has been fixed, in order that those who would pass from here to you may not be able, and none may cross from there to us." And he said, "Then I beg you, father, to send him to my father's house, for I have five brothers, so that he may warn them, lest they also come into this place of torment." But Abraham said, "They have Moses and the prophets; let them hear them." And he said, "No, father Abraham; but if some one goes to them from the dead, they will repent." He said to him, "If they do not hear Moses and the prophets, neither will they be convinced if some one should rise from the dead."

Luke 16:19-31

. . . Why do you trouble the woman? For she has done a beautiful thing to me. For you always have the poor with you, but you will not always have me. In pouring this ointment on my body she has done it to prepare me for burial. Truly, I say to you, wherever this gospel is preached in the whole world, what she has done will be told in memory of her.

Matt. 26:10-13

. . . Let her alone; why do you trouble her? She has done a beautiful thing to me. For you always have the poor with you, and whenever you will, you can do good to them; but you will not always have me. She has done what she could; she has anointed my body beforehand for burying. And truly, I say to you, wherever the gospel is preached in the whole world, what she has done will be told in memory of her.

Mark 14:6-9

. . . Let her alone, let her keep it for the day of my burial. The poor you always have with you, but you do not always have me.

John 12:7-8

. . . Truly, I say to you, it will be hard for a rich man to enter the kingdom of heaven. Again I tell you, it is easier for a camel to go through **wealth** the eye of a needle than for a rich man to enter the kingdom of God. . . . With men this is impossible, but with God all things are possible. **God**

Matt. 19:23-26

. . . How hard it will be for those who have riches to enter the kingdom of God! . . . Children, how hard it is to enter the kingdom of God! **kingdom** It is easier for a camel to go through the **of God** eye of a needle than for a rich man to enter the kingdom of God. . . . With men it is impossible, but not with God; for all things are possible with God.

Mark 10:23-27

. . . How hard it is for those who have riches to enter the kingdom of God! For it is easier for a camel to go through the eye of a needle than for a rich man to enter the kingdom of God. . . . What is impossible with men is possible with God.

Luke 18:24-27

. . . Take these things away; you shall not make my Father's house a house of trade.

John 2:16

. . . Truly, truly, I say to you, you seek me, not because you saw signs, but because you ate your fill of the loaves. Do not labor for the food which perishes, but for the food which endures to eternal life, which the Son of man will give to you; for on him has God the Father set his seal.

John 6:26-27

. . . It is more blessed to give than to receive.

Acts 20:35

Passion

(CRUCIFIXION)

Scholars tell us that in the beginning of the Christian Church, the center of attention for the disciples was the crucifixion and resurrection of Jesus. Only later was their attention focused on his teaching. Thus Paul, the first among the New Testament writers, says very little about the teachings of Jesus. Scholars attribute this to the probability that Paul's hearers were already familiar with the words of Jesus that were presumably circulating in some written form, usually collections of sayings such as we have in the Sermon on the Mount (Matt. 5,6,7). And surely there was much oral transmission of Jesus' words at the same time.

But the fact remains that central to the preaching of the early disciples were the crucifixion and resurrection. The power in this mighty drama stirred the hearts of those who heard. According to the book of Acts, three thousand converts were made as the result of Peter's first sermon on the day of Pentecost. (Acts 2)

By his voluntary self-sacrifice Jesus illustrated one of his own sayings: "Greater love has no man than this, that a man lay down his life for his friends." (John

15:13) Supreme example of the divine love, the crucifixion moved the disciples to tell of Christ and his passion and death as they moved outward from Palestine to the other countries of the world. In each of the gospels Jesus announces his approaching death to the disciples, yet they cannot understand or believe he will have to bear such suffering. They could not see that final victory is in God's hands.

* * *

. . . The Son of man is to be delivered into the hands of men, and they will kill him, and he will be raised on the third day.

Matt. 17:22-23

. . . The Son of man will be delivered into the hands of men, and they will kill him; and when he is killed, after three days he will rise.

Mark 9:31

. . . Let these words sink into your ears; for the Son of man is to be delivered into the hands of men.

Luke 9:44

. . . Behold, we are going up to Jerusalem; and the Son of man will be delivered to the chief priests and scribes, and they will condemn him to death, and deliver him to the Gentiles to be mocked and scourged and crucified, and he will be raised on the third day.

Matt. 20:18-19

. . . Behold, we are going up to Jerusalem; and the Son of man will be delivered to the chief priests and the scribes, and they will condemn him to death, and deliver him to the Gentiles; and they will mock him, and spit upon him, and scourge him, and kill him; and after three days he will rise.

Mark 10:33-34

O Jerusalem, Jerusalem, killing the prophets and stoning those who are sent to you! How often would I have gathered your children together as a hen gathers her brood under her wings, and you would not! Behold, your house is forsaken and desolate. For I tell you, you will not see me again, until you say, "Blessed be he who comes in the name of the Lord."

Matt. 23:37-39

. . . Go and tell that fox, "Behold, I cast out demons and perform cures today and tomorrow, and the third day I finish my course. Nevertheless I must go on my way today and tomorrow and the day following; for it cannot be that a prophet should perish away from Jerusalem." O Jerusalem, Jerusalem, killing the prophets and stoning those who are sent to you! How often would I have gathered your children together as a hen gathers her brood under her wings, and you would not! Behold, your house is forsaken. And I tell you, you will not see me until you say, "Blessed is he who comes in the name of the Lord!"

Luke 13:32-35

. . . Behold, we are going up to Jerusalem, and everything that is written of the Son of man by the prophets will be accomplished. For he will be delivered to the Gentiles, and will be mocked and shamefully treated and spit upon, they will scourge him and kill him, and on the third day he will rise.

Luke 18:31-33

. . . You see all these, do you not? Truly, I say to you, there will not be left here one stone upon another, that will not be thrown down.

Matt. 24:2

. . . You know that after two days the Passover is coming, and the Son of man will be delivered up to be crucified.

Matt. 26:2

. . . You have said so.

Matt. 27:11

. . . Eli, Eli, lama sabachthani? [that is, My God, my God, why hast thou forsaken me?]

Matt. 27:46

. . . Judas, would you betray the Son of man with a kiss?

Luke 22:48

. . . No more of this!

Luke 22:51

. . . Have you come out as against a robber, with swords and clubs? When I was with you day after day in the temple, you did not lay hands on me. But this is your hour, and the power of darkness.

Luke 22:52-53

. . . If I tell you, you will not believe; and if I ask you will not answer. But from now on the Son of man shall be seated at the right hand of the power of God. . . . You say that I am.

Luke 22:67-70

. . . You have said so.

Luke 23:3

. . . Truly, I say to you, today you will be with me in Paradise.

Luke 23:43

. . . I am not speaking of you all; I know whom I have chosen; it is that the scripture may be fulfilled, "He who ate my bread has lifted his heel against me." I tell you this now, before it takes place, that when it does take place you may believe that I am he. Truly, truly, I say to you, he who receives any one whom I send receives me; and he who receives me receives him who sent me.

. . . Truly, truly, I say to you, one of you will betray me. . . . It is he to whom I shall give this morsel when

I have dipped it. . . . What you are going to do, do quickly.

John 13:18-27

. . . Whom do you seek? . . . I am he. . . . Whom do you seek? . . . I told you that I am he; so, if you seek me, let these men go. . . . Put your sword into its sheath; shall I not drink the cup which the Father has given me?

John 18:4-11

. . . I have spoken openly to the world; I have always taught in synagogues and in the temple, where all Jews come together; I have said nothing secretly. Why do you ask me? Ask those who have heard me, what I said to them; they know what I said. . . . If I have spoken wrongly, bear witness to the wrong; but if I have spoken rightly, why do you strike me?

John 18:20-23

. . . Do you say this of your own accord, or did others say it to you about me? . . . My kingship is not of this world; if my kingship were of this world, my servants would fight, that I might not be handed over to the Jews; but my kingship is not from the world. . . . You say that I am a king. For this **kingdom of God** I was born, and for this I have come into the world, to bear witness to the truth. Every one who is of the truth hears my voice.

John 18:34-37

. . . You would have no power over me unless it had been given you from above; therefore he who delivered me to you has the greater sin.

John 19:11

. . . Woman, behold your son! . . . Behold your mother! . . . I thirst. . . . It is finished.

John 19:26-30

. . . Go into the city to such a one, and say to him, "The Teacher says, My time is at hand; I will keep the passover at your house with my disciples."

Matt. 26:18

. . . Truly, I say to you, one of you will betray me. . . . He who has dipped his hand in the dish with me, will betray me. The Son of man goes as it is written of him, but woe to that man by whom the Son of man is betrayed! It would have been better for that man if he had not been born. . . . You have said so.

. . . Take, eat; this is my body. . . . Drink of it, all of you; for this is my blood of the covenant, which is poured out for many for the forgiveness of sins. I tell you I shall not drink again of this fruit of the vine until that day when I drink it new with you in my Father's kingdom. . . . You will all fall away because of me this night; for it is **kingdom of God** written, "I will strike the shepherd, and the sheep of the flock will be scattered." But after I am raised up, I will go before you to Galilee. . . . Truly, I say to you, this very night, before the cock crows, you will deny me three times.

Matt. 26:21-34

. . . Are you still sleeping and taking your rest? Behold, the hour is at hand, and the Son of man is betrayed into the hands of sinners. Rise, let us be going; see, my betrayer is at hand. . . . Friend, why are you here? . . . Put your sword back into its place; for all who take the sword will perish by the sword. Do you think that I cannot appeal to my Father, **peace** and he will at once send me more than twelve legions of angels? But how then should the scriptures be fulfilled, that it must be so? . . . Have you come out as against a robber, with swords and clubs to capture me? Day after day I sat in the temple teaching, and you did not seize me. But all this has taken place, that the scriptures of the prophets might be fulfilled. . . .

You have said so. But I tell you, hereafter you will see the Son of man seated at the right hand of Power, and coming on the clouds of heaven.

Matt. 26:45-64

. . . This is my body which is for you. Do this in remembrance of me. . . . This cup is the new covenant in my blood. Do this, as often as you drink it, in remembrance of me.

1 Cor. 11:24-25

Prayer

Jesus took the need of prayer for granted. Prayer was a part of the everyday life of the Jewish people. But Jesus saw that much of the praying of his day was for show, and he warned his disciples to pray, not on the street corners as the hypocrites did, but in secret.

There is little likelihood in our time that people will pray on street corners to show off their religiousness, but there is the danger that our prayers may become thoughtless, nonsensical repetitions which "rise no higher than our heads."

Prayer is conversation with God. It may be formal, as in the written prayers recited in church, or it may be the intimate pouring out of the individual's heart in the secret of his hiding place. In either case, it is communication with God.

Jesus taught his disciples to pray when he gave them "The Lord's Prayer," which serves as an example for our prayers.

If prayer was essential in his life for the great tasks he had to perform, can we believe that we can carry on as responsible Christians without it?

Jesus said prayers will be answered since God's will is always for our good. Prayer opens our lives to receive his goodness, for help in meeting the needs of our everyday lives. No one can imagine the help available through prayer unless he has experienced it himself.

Jesus did not, however, receive everything he asked for. While praying in the garden of Gethsemane, he asked to be relieved of the cross—"let this cup pass from me"—but was not. However God did give Jesus victory over death in his resurrection. *This* was not the answer he asked for, but a better one. Like Jesus, we should pray, "Not my will, but thine be done."

Real prayer takes time. Jesus found it by going out to the mountains early in the morning. We, too, need a time and a quiet place apart for this most important communication of all—communication with God.

* * *

And when you pray, you must not be like the hypocrites; for they love to stand and pray in the synagogues and at the street corners, that they may be seen by men. Truly, I say to **hypocrites** you, they have their reward. But when you pray, go into your room and shut the door and pray to your Father who is in secret; and your Father who sees in secret will reward you.

And in praying do not heap up empty phrases as the Gentiles do; for they think that they will be heard for their many words. Do not be like them, for your Father knows what you need before you ask him. Pray then like this:

> Our Father who art in heaven,
> Hallowed be thy name.
> Thy kingdom come,
> Thy will be done,
>   On earth as it is in heaven.
> Give us this day our daily bread;
> And forgive us our debts,
>   As we also have forgiven our debtors,
> And lead us not into temptation,
>   But deliver us from evil.

Matt. 6:5-13

. . . When you pray, say:

Father, hallowed be thy name. Thy kingdom come. Give us each day our daily bread; and forgive us our sins, for we ourselves forgive every one who is indebted to us; and lead us not into temptation.

Luke 11:2-4

Ask, and it will be given you; seek, and you will find; knock, and it will be opened to you. For every one who asks receives, and he who seeks finds, and to him who knocks it will be opened. Or what man of you, if his son asks him for bread, will give him a stone? Or if he asks for a fish, will give him a serpent? If you then, who are evil, know how to give good gifts to your children, how much more will your Father who is in heaven give good things to those who ask him!

Matt. 7:7-11

. . . Which of you who has a friend will go to him at midnight and say to him, "Friend, lend me three loaves; for a friend of mine has arrived on a journey, and I have nothing to set before him"; **God** and he will answer from within, "Do not bother me; the door is now shut, and my children are with me in bed; I cannot get up and give you anything"? I tell you, though he will not get up and give him anything because he is his friend, yet because of his importunity he will rise and give him whatever he needs. And I tell you, Ask, and it will be given you; seek, and you will find; knock, and it will be opened to you. For every one who asks receives, and he who seeks finds, and to him who knocks it will be opened. What father among you, if his son asks for a fish, will instead of a fish give him a serpent; or if he asks for an egg, will give him a scorpion? If you then, who are evil, know how to give good gifts to your children, **Holy Spirit** how much more will the heavenly Father give the Holy Spirit to those who ask him!

Luke 11:5-13

. . . Truly, I say to you, whatever you bind on earth shall be bound in heaven, and whatever you loose on earth shall be loosed in heaven. **heaven** Again I say to you, if two of you agree on earth about anything they ask, it will be done for them by my Father in heaven. For where two or three are gathered in my name, there am I in the midst of **God** them.

Matt. 18:18-20

. . . It is written, "My house shall be called a house of prayer"; but you make it a den of robbers.

Matt. 21:13

. . . Is it not written, "My house shall be called a house of prayer for all the nations"? But you have made it a den of robbers.

Mark 11:17

. . . It is written, "My house shall be a house of prayer"; but you have made it a den of robbers.

Luke 19:46

. . . Sit here, while I go yonder and pray. . . . My soul is very sorrowful, even to death; remain here, and watch with me. . . . My Father, if it be possible, let this cup pass from me; nevertheless, not as I will, but as thou wilt. . . . So, could you not watch with me one hour? Watch and pray that you may not enter into temptation; the spirit indeed is willing, but the flesh is weak. . . . My Father, if this cannot pass unless I drink it, thy will be done.

Matt. 26:36-42

. . . My soul is very sorrowful, even to death; remain here, and watch. . . . Abba, Father, all things are possible to thee; remove this cup from me; yet not what I will, but what thou wilt. . . . Simon, are you asleep? Could you not watch one hour? Watch and pray that you may not enter into temptation; the spirit indeed is willing, but the flesh is weak.

Mark 14:34-38

. . . Pray that you may not enter into temptation. . . . Father, if thou art willing, remove this cup from me; nevertheless not my will, but thine, be done. . . . Why do you sleep? Rise and pray that you may not enter into temptation.

Luke 22:40-46

Now is my soul troubled. And what shall I say, "Father, save me from this hour"? No, for this purpose I have come to this hour. Father, glorify thy name.

John 12:27-28

. . . Whatever you ask in my name, I will do it, that the Father may be glorified in the Son; if you ask anything in my name, I will do it.

John 14:13-14

. . . Two men went up into the temple to pray, one a Pharisee and the other a tax collector. The Pharisee stood and prayed thus with himself, "God, I thank thee that I am not like other men, extortioners, unjust, adulterers, or even like this tax collector. I fast twice a week, I give tithes of all that I get." But the tax collector, standing far off, would not even lift up his eyes to heaven, but beat his breast, saying, "God be merciful to me a sinner!" I tell you, this man went down to his house justified rather than the other; for every one who exalts himself will be **forgiveness** humbled, but he who humbles himself will be exalted.

Luke 18:10-14

Resurrection

The resurrection is God's victory over the evil of the crucifixion. Without the resurrection, Jesus would still be a great teacher, but there would be no Christian religion. There might have been a Jewish sect called the Jesus Party, but it hardly would have moved the disciples to "go into all the world to preach the gospel." Christianity would not have conquered the Roman empire. There would have been no Christian Church.

It was their belief in the risen Lord which stirred the early Christians to heroic efforts, to missionary witnessing, to martyrdom. So today the teachings of Jesus, potent as they are, lack power without reference to the resurrection. It was the resurrection which convinced early Christians that He was the Son of God.

Most of the passages in this section are words Jesus spoke during the forty days of his appearance after the resurrection. Note that all of his appearances are to his friends; he did not appear to his enemies.

The four gospel accounts are each a little different. The significance of these differences gives scholars much opportunity for debate; however, all four gospels agree that Jesus rose from the dead. Paul, too, in the earliest written account that we have of the resurrection (I Cor. 15:3-8) testifies to the fact of the resurrection.

This victory over death gives us hope for our lives in the same way in which it gave hope to Paul, to Peter, James, John, Thomas and the others who followed Christ.

* * *

. . . Tell no one the vision, until the Son of man is raised from the dead.

Matt. 17:9

. . . Hail! . . . Do not be afraid; go and tell my brethren to go to Galilee, and there they will see me.

Matt. 28:9-10

. . . What is this conversation which you are holding with each other as you walk? . . . What things? . . . O foolish men, and slow of heart to believe all that the prophets have spoken! Was it not necessary that the Christ should suffer these things and enter into his glory?

Luke 24:17-26

. . . Why are you troubled, and why do questionings rise in your hearts? See my hands and my feet, that it is I myself; handle me, and see; for a spirit has not flesh and bones as you see that I have. . . . Have you anything here to eat?

Luke 24:38-41

. . . These are my words which I spoke to you, while I was still with you, that everything written about me in the law of Moses and the prophets and the psalms must be fulfilled. . . . Thus it is written, **evangelism** that Christ should suffer and on the third day rise from the dead, and that repentance and forgiveness of sins should be preached in his name to all nations, beginning from Jerusalem. You **Holy Spirit** are witnesses of these things. And behold, I send the promise of my Father upon you; but stay in the city, until you are clothed with power from on high.

Luke 24:44-49

. . . Destroy this temple, and in three days I will raise it up.

John 2:19

. . . Woman, why are you weeping? Whom do you seek? . . . Mary. . . . Do not hold me, for I have not yet ascended to the Father; but go to my brethren and say to them, I am ascending to my Father and your Father, to my God and your God.

John 20:15-17

Peace be with you. . . . Put your finger here, and see my hands; and put out your hand, and place it in my side; do not be faithless, but believing. . . . Have you believed because you have seen me? Blessed are those who have not seen and yet believe.

John 20:26-29

. . . Children, have you any fish? . . . Cast the net on the right side of the boat, and you will find some. . . . Bring some of the fish that you have just caught. . . . Come and have breakfast.

John 21:5-12

Sin

In the teachings of Jesus, sin is real, not a hazy concept described as weakness due to some unfortunate childhood experiences. Jesus saw sin as a fact of life, the act of disobeying God. Man's disobedience began in the Garden of Eden; it continues even now whenever men live contrary to God's will.

As we see in the Old Testament, the reality of sin was deeply rooted in Jewish faith. But Jesus injected a new meaning into the term when he emphasized the importance of the *thoughts* of man. It is the hidden desires of man which comprise the springs of his actions. An excellent example of this is the first passage in this section, concerning adultery. Jesus made his point very sharp: the sin of adultery begins in desire. "Every one who looks at a woman lustfully has already committed adultery with her in his heart."

On another occasion Jesus put the same principle in different words, "Not that which goeth into the mouth defileth a man but that which cometh out of the mouth. . . ." Thus sin begins in the thoughts and emotions and they become the "father of the deed."

Another point Jesus made that was revolutionary to his time is that God continues to love the sinner. Jesus went on to point out that misfortune and natural disaster are not visited on people as a result of sin.

161

Jesus rejected the old idea that sickness was a direct result of sin; he said that the rain falls "on the just and on the unjust."

But to Jesus sin was serious for it broke the intimate relationship between God and man. Paul spoke strongly about sin in these words, "the wages of sin is death."

When we repent of our sins, God's forgiveness becomes available to cleanse us from guilt and give us a new start in life.

*　*　*

You have heard that it was said, "You shall not commit adultery." But I say to you that every one who looks at a woman lustfully has already committed adultery with her in his heart. If your right eye causes you to sin, pluck it out and throw it away; it is better that you lose one of your members than that your whole body be thrown into hell. And if your **hell** right hand causes you to sin, cut it off and throw it away; it is better that you lose one of your members than that your whole body go into hell.

Matt. 5:27-30

Again you have heard that it was said to the men of old, "You shall not swear falsely, but shall perform to the Lord what you have sworn." But I say to you, Do not swear at all, either by heaven, **swearing** for it is the throne of God, or by the earth, for it is his footstool, or by Jerusalem, for it is the city of the great King. And do not swear by your head, for you cannot make one hair white or black. Let what you say be simply "Yes" or "No"; anything more than this comes from evil.

Matt. 5:33-37

. . . Those who are well have no need of a physician, but those who are sick. Go and learn what this means, "I desire mercy, and not sacrifice." For I came not to call the righteous, but sinners.

Matt. 9:12-13

. . . Those who are well have no need of a physician, but those who are sick; I came not to call the righteous, but sinners. *healing*

Mark 2:17

. . . Those who are well have no need of a physician, but those who are sick; I have not come to call the righteous, but sinners to repentance.

Luke 5:31-32

But to what shall I compare this generation? It is like children sitting in the market places and calling to their playmates.

"We piped to you, and you did not dance;
we wailed, and you did not mourn."

For John came neither eating nor drinking, and they say, "He has a demon"; the Son of man came eating and drinking, and they say, "Behold, a glutton and a drunkard, a friend of tax collectors and sinners!" Yet wisdom is justified by her deeds.

Matt. 11:16-19

To what then shall I compare the men of this generation and what are they like? They are like children sitting in the market place and calling to one another,

"We piped to you, and you did not dance;
we wailed, and you did not weep."

For John the Baptist has come eating no bread and drinking no wine; and you say, "He has a demon." The Son of man has come eating and drinking; and you say, "Behold, a glutton and a drunkard, a friend of tax collectors and sinners!" Yet wisdom is justified by all her children.

Luke 7:31-35

. . . Every kingdom divided against itself is laid waste, and no city or house divided against itself will stand; and if Satan casts out Satan, he is divided against himself; how then will his kingdom stand? And if I cast out demons by Beelzebul, by whom do your sons cast them out? Therefore they shall be your judges. But if it is by the Spirit of God that I cast out demons, then the kingdom of God has come upon you. Or how can one enter a **kingdom of God** strong man's house and plunder his goods, unless he first binds the strong man? Then indeed he may plunder his house. He who is not with me is against me, and he who does not gather with me scatters. Therefore I tell you, every sin and blasphemy will be forgiven men, but the blasphemy against the Spirit will not be forgiven. And whoever says a word against the Son of man will be for- **Holy Spirit** given; but whoever speaks against the Holy Spirit will not be forgiven, either in this age or in the age to come.

Either make the tree good, and its fruit good; or make the tree bad, and its fruit bad; for the tree is known by its fruit. You brood of vipers! how can you speak good, when you are evil? For out of the abundance of the heart the mouth speaks. The good man out of his good treasure brings forth good, and the evil man out of his evil treasure brings forth evil. I tell you, on the day of judgment men will render account for every careless word they utter; for by your words you will be justified, and by your words you will be condemned.

Matt. 12:25-37

. . . How can Satan cast out Satan? If a kingdom is divided against itself, that kingdom cannot stand. And if a house is divided against itself, that house will not be able to stand. And if Satan has risen up against himself and is divided, he cannot stand, but is coming to an end. But no one can enter a strong man's house and plunder his goods, unless he first binds the strong man; then indeed he may plunder his house.

Truly, I say to you, all sins will be forgiven the sons of men, and whatever blasphemies they utter; but who-

ever blasphemes against the Holy Spirit never has forgiveness, but is guilty of an eternal sin.

Mark 3:23-30

. . . Every kingdom divided against itself is laid
waste, and house falls upon house. And if Satan also is
divided against himself, how will his kingdom stand?
For you say that I cast out demons by Beelzebul. And if
I cast out demons by Beelzebul, by whom do your sons
cast them out? Therefore they shall be your judges.
But if it is by the finger of God that I cast out demons,
then the kingdom of God has come upon you. When a
strong man, fully armed, guards his own palace, his
goods are in peace; but when one stronger than he
assails him and overcomes him, he takes away his armor
in which he trusted, and divides his spoil. He who is
not with me is against me, and he who does not gather
with me scatters.

Luke 11:17-23

. . . An evil and adulterous generation seeks for a
sign; but no sign shall be given to it except the sign of
the prophet Jonah. For as Jonah was three days and
three nights in the belly of the whale, so will the Son
of man be three days and three nights in the heart of
the earth. The men of Nineveh will arise at the judgment with this generation and condemn it; for they repented at the preaching of Jonah, and behold, something greater than Jonah is here. The Queen of the
South will arise at the judgment with this generation
and condemn it; for she came from the ends of the
earth to hear the wisdom of Solomon, and behold,
something greater than Solomon is here.

When the unclean spirit has gone out of a man, he
passes through waterless places seeking rest, but he finds
none. Then he says, "I will return to my house from
which I came." And when he comes he finds it empty,
swept, and put in order. Then he goes and brings with
him seven other spirits more evil than himself, and

they enter and dwell there; and the last state of that man becomes worse than the first. So shall it be also with this evil generation.

Matt. 12:39-45

. . . This generation is an evil generation; it seeks a sign, but no sign shall be given to it except the sign of Jonah. For as Jonah became a sign to the men of Nineveh, so will the Son of man be to this generation. The queen of the South will arise at the judgment with the men of this generation and condemn them; for she came from the ends of the earth to hear the wisdom of Solomon, and behold, something greater than Solomon is here. The men of Nineveh will arise at the judgment with this generation and condemn it; for they repented at the preaching of Jonah, and behold, something greater than Jonah is here.

No one after lighting a lamp puts it in a cellar or under a bushel, but on a stand, that those who enter may see the light. Your eye is the lamp of your body; when your eye is sound, your whole body is full of light; but when it is not sound, your body is full of darkness. Therefore be careful lest the light in you be darkness.

Luke 11:29-36

. . . Get behind me, Satan! You are a hindrance to me; for you are not on the side of God, but of men.

Matt. 16:23

. . . And why do you transgress the commandment of God for the sake of your tradition? For God commanded, "Honor your father and your mother," and, "He who speaks evil of father or mother, let him surely die." But you say, "If any one tells his father or his mother, What you would **hypocrites** have gained from me is given to God, he need not honor his father." So, for the sake of your tradition, you have made void the word of God. You hypocrites! Well did Isaiah prophesy of you, when he said:

"This people honors me with their lips,
 but their heart is far from me;
 in vain do they worship me,
 teaching as doctrines the precepts of men."

. . . Hear and understand: not what goes into the mouth defiles a man, but what comes out of the mouth, this defiles a man. . . . Every plant which my heavenly Father has not planted will be rooted up. Let them alone; they are blind guides. And if a blind man leads a blind man, both will fall into a pit. . . . Are you also still without understanding? Do you not see that whatever goes into the mouth passes into the stomach, and so passes on? But what comes out of the mouth proceeds from the heart, and this defiles a man. For out of the heart come evil thoughts, murder, adultery, fornication, theft, false witness, slander. These are what defile a man; but to eat with unwashed hands does not defile a man.

Matt. 15:3-20

. . . Well did Isaiah prophesy of you hypocrites, as it is written,

"This people honors me with their lips,
 but their heart is far from me;
 in vain do they worship me,
 teaching as doctrines the precepts of men."

You leave the commandment of God, and hold fast the tradition of men.

. . . You have a fine way of rejecting the commandment of God, in order to keep your tradition! For Moses said, "Honor your father and your mother"; and, "He who speaks evil of father or mother, let him surely die"; but you say, "If a man tell his father or his mother, What you would have gained from me is Corban" (that is, given to God)—then you no longer permit him to do anything for his father or mother, thus making void the word of God through your tradition which you hand on. And many such things you do.

. . . Hear me, all of you, and understand: there is nothing outside a man which by going into him can defile him; but the things which come out of a man are what defile him. . . . Then are you also without understanding? Do you not see that whatever goes into a man from outside cannot defile him, since it enters, not his heart but his stomach, and so passes on? (Thus he declared all foods clean.) . . . What comes out of a man is what defiles a man. For from within, out of the heart of man, come evil thoughts, fornication, theft, murder, adultery, coveting, wickedness, deceit, licentiousness, envy, slander, pride, foolishness. All these evil things come from within, and they defile a man.

Mark 7:6-23

. . . Can a blind man lead a blind man? Will they not both fall into a pit?

Luke 6:39

. . . When it is evening, you say, "It will be fair weather; for the sky is red." And in the morning, "It will be stormy today, for the sky is red and threatening." You know how to interpret the appearance of the sky, but you cannot interpret the signs of the times. An evil and adulterous generation seeks for a sign, but no sign shall be given to it except the sign of Jonah.

Matt. 16:2-4

. . . Why does this generation seek a sign? Truly, I say to you, no sign shall be given to this generation.

Mark 8:12

Woe to the world for temptations to sin! For it is necessary that temptations come, but woe to the man by whom the temptation comes! And if your hand or your foot causes you to sin, cut it off and throw it from you; it is better for you to enter life maimed or lame than with two hands or two feet to be thrown into the eternal fire. And if your eye causes you to sin, pluck it out and throw it from you; it is better for you to enter life with one eye than with two eyes to be thrown into the hell of fire.

See that you do not despise one of these little ones; for I tell you that in heaven their angels always behold the face of my Father who is in heaven.

Matt. 18:7-11

. . . Temptations to sin are sure to come; but woe to him by whom they come! It would be better for him if a millstone were hung round his neck and he were cast into the sea, than that he should cause one of these little ones to sin.

Luke 17:1-2

. . . Do not forbid him; for no one who does a mighty work in my name will be able soon after to speak evil of me. For he that is not against us is for us. For truly, I say to you, whoever gives **rewards** you a cup of water to drink because you bear the name of Christ, will by no means lose his reward.

Whoever causes one of these little ones who believe in me to sin, it would be better for him if a great millstone were hung round his neck and he were thrown into the sea. And if your **children** hand causes you to sin, cut it off; it is better for you to enter life maimed than with two hands to go to hell, to the unquenchable fire. And if your foot causes you to sin, cut it off; it is better for you to enter life lame than with two feet to be thrown into hell. **hell** And if your eye causes you to sin, pluck it out; it is better for you to enter the kingdom of God with one eye than with two eyes to be thrown into hell, where their worm does not die, and the fire is not quenched. For every one will be salted with fire. Salt is good; but if the salt has lost its saltness, how will you season it? Have salt in yourselves, and be at **peace** peace with one another.

Mark 9:39-50

. . . Is it not written, "My house shall be called a house of prayer for all the nations"? But you have made it a den of robbers.

Mark 11:17

. . . Let him who is without sin among you be the first to throw a stone at her. . . . Woman, where are they? Has no one condemned you? . . . Neither do I condemn you; go, and do not sin again.

John 8:7-11

. . . I go away, and you will seek me and die in your sin; where I am going, you cannot come. . . . You are from below, I am from above; you are of this world, I am not of this world. I told you that you would die in your sins, for you will die in your sins unless you believe that I am he.

John 8:21-24

. . . Truly, truly, I say to you, every one who commits sin is a slave to sin. The slave does not continue in the house for ever; the son continues for ever. So if the Son makes you free, you will be free indeed. I know that you are descendants of Abraham; yet you seek to kill me, because my word finds no place in you. I speak of what I have seen with my Father, and you do what you have heard from your father.
. . . If you were Abraham's children, you would do what Abraham did, but now you seek to kill me, a man who has told you the truth which I heard from God; this is not what Abraham did. You do what your father did. . . . If God were your Father, you would love me, for I proceeded and came forth from God; I came not of my own accord, but he sent me. Why do you not understand what I say? It is because you cannot bear to hear my word. You are of your father the devil, and your will is to do your father's desires. He was a murderer from the beginning, and has nothing to do with the truth, because there is no truth in him.

When he lies, he speaks according to his own nature, for he is a liar and the father of lies. But, because I tell the truth, you do not believe me. Which of you convicts me of sin? If I tell the truth, why do you not believe me? He who is of God hears the words of God; the reason why you do not hear them is that you are not of God.

John 8:34-47

. . . It was not that this man sinned, or his parents, but that the works of God might be made manifest in him. We must work the works of him who sent me, while it is day; night comes, when no one can work. As long as I am in the world, I am the light of the world. . . . Go, wash in the pool of Siloam (which means Sent).

John 9:3-7

. . . For judgment I came into this world, that those who do not see may see, and that those who see may become blind. . . . If you were **judgment** blind, you would have no guilt; but now that you say, "We see," your guilt remains.

John 9:39-41

. . . Where I am going you cannot follow me now; but you shall follow afterward. . . . Will you lay down your life for me? Truly, truly, I say to you, the cock will not crow, till you have denied me three times.

John 13:36-38

If the world hates you, know that it has hated me before it hated you. If you were of the world, the world would love its own; but because you **hate** are not of the world, but I chose you out of the world, therefore the world hates you. Remember the word that I said to you, "A servant is not greater than his master." If they persecuted me, they will persecute you; if they kept my word, they **persecution** will keep yours also. But all this they will do to you on my account, because they do not know him who sent me. If I had not come and spoken to them, they would not have sin; but now they have no excuse for their sin. He who hates me hates my Father also. If I had not done among them the works which no one else did, they would not have sin; but now they have seen and hated both me and my Father. It is to fufil the word that is written in their law, "They hated me without a cause."

John 15:18-25

. . . Do you think that these Galileans were worse sinners than all the other Galileans, because they suffered thus? I tell you, No; but unless you repent you will all likewise perish. Or those eighteen upon whom the tower in Siloam fell and killed them, do you think that they were worse offenders than all the others who dwelt in Jerusalem? I tell you, No; but unless you repent you will all likewise perish.

Luke 13:2-5

. . . You are those who justify yourselves before men, but God knows your hearts; for what is exalted among men is an abomination in the sight of God.

The law and the prophets were until John; since then the good news of the kingdom of God is preached, and every one enters it violently. But it is easier for heaven and earth to pass away, than for one dot of the law to become void.

kingdom of God

Luke 16:15-17

Miscellaneous

There are a few passages containing Jesus' words that do not fall into any of the subject headings used in this book. Since these sayings of Jesus are important they are included to give a complete text of all the words in the New Testament attributed to him.

Here are five passages, each on a different subject. According to the gospel of John, there were many more words of Jesus that are not recorded in the New Testament. Some of these are found in such recently discovered manuscripts as the Gospel of Thomas. There may be still other manuscripts coming to light from the darkness of desert caves, yet it seems that we possess in the New Testament all the words of Jesus that we need in order to learn of God and his will.

The character of Jesus' life and teachings is well established. Our chief obligation is not to discover more words of Jesus, but to live by the words we have.

* * *

JOHN THE BAPTIST

. . . Let it be so now; for thus it is fitting for us to fulfil all righteousness.

Matt. 3:15

. . . What did you go out into the wilderness to behold? A reed shaken by the wind? Why then did you go out? To see a man clothed in soft raiment? Behold, those who wear soft raiment are in kings' houses. Why then did you go out? To see a prophet? Yes, I tell you, and more than a prophet. This is he of whom it is written,

> "Behold, I send my messenger before thy face,
> who shall prepare thy way before thee."

Truly, I say to you, among those born of women there has risen no one greater than John the Baptist; yet he who is least in the kingdom of heaven is greater than he. From the days of John the Baptist until now the kingdom of heaven has suffered violence, and men of violence take it by force. For all the prophets and the law prophesied until John; and if you are willing to accept it, he is Elijah who is to come. He who has ears to hear, let him hear.

Matt. 11:7-15

PREPARATION FOR THE TRIUMPHAL ENTRY INTO JERUSALEM

. . . Go into the village opposite you, and immediately you will find an ass tied, and a colt with her; untie them and bring them to me. If any one says anything to you, you shall say, "The Lord has need of them," and he will send them immediately.

Matt. 21:2-3

TO THE CHIEF PRIESTS AND SCRIBES

. . . Yes; have you never read, "Out of the mouth of babes and sucklings thou hast brought perfect praise"?

Matt. 21:16

TURNING WATER INTO WINE

. . . O woman, what have you to do with me? My hour has not yet come. . . . Fill the jars with water. . . . Now draw some out, and take it to the steward of the feast.

John 2:4-8

IN THE GARDEN OF GETHSEMANE

. . . Of those whom thou gavest me I lost not one.

John 18:9